Memorable Dogs

146

Memorable Dogs AN ANTHOLOGY

BENJAMIN T. SPENCER, Editor

Helen Crider Smith, Associate Editor

HARPER & ROW, PUBLISHERS, New York
CAMBRIDGE, PHILADELPHIA, SAN FRANCISCO, LONDON
MEXICO CITY, SÃO PAULO, SINGAPORE, SYDNEY
1817

■ *To Virginia Morrison Spencer*

Copyright acknowledgments begin on page 197.

FIRST EDITION

Designer: Barbara DuPree Knowles

Library of Congress Cataloging in Publication Data
Main entry under title:
Memorable dogs.
    1. Dogs—Literary collections.   2. English literature.   3. American literature.   I. Spencer, Benjamin Townley.   II. Smith, Helen Crider.
PR1111.D6M45   1985   820'.8'036   84-48626
ISBN 0-06-015440-3

---

85 86 87 88 89 HC 10 9 8 7 6 5 4 3 2 1

Contents

Acknowledgments

One of the obviously valid ways of selecting "memorable dogs" is to ask friends and acquaintances what dogs they remember from their reading. The answers we received to this question included not only specific dogs but also clues which led to further discoveries. By this process some of the most interesting canine characters came to be included in this anthology. Among those who provided such assistance or helpful clarification of the data are Frank Buske, Richard Elias, Edwin Folsom, Patricia Ross French, Kathryn Motz Hunter, Joy Lee King, Lyman Leathers, Donald Lateiner, James Morrison, Mildred Newcomb, Amy Roebuck, Kadell Shanklin, Nancy Caldwell Sorel, Ella Stone Spencer, Susan Pomeroy Wyler, and Clareene Motz Wharry.

Special thanks are due to William Farragher and Harry Wood for bestowing on us for three years an informative mass of canine data which broadened and deepened our understanding of the changing status of dogs in society and art. They furnished numerous candidates for the anthology and noted correlations between verbal portraits of dogs and those in painting and sculpture in certain eras. Their unflagging interest in the project was reassuring, and their many-faceted comments consistently valuable. Special thanks are also due to Gordon Smith for his interest and encouragement from the outset and for helping to facilitate the preparation of the many copies which were used in the polishing of the text.

Introduction

"Various and wonderful, in all ages, have been the actions of dogs; and were I to collect, from poets and historians, the many passages that make honourable mention of them, I should compose a work much too large and voluminous for the patience of any modern reader. . . . And can we, without the basest ingratitude, think ill of an animal that has ever honoured mankind with his company and friendship, from the beginning of the world to the present moment? While all other creatures are in a state of enmity with us; some flying into woods and wildernesses to escape our tyranny, and others requiring to be restrained with bridles and fences in close confinement; dogs alone enter into voluntary friendship with us, and of their own accord make their residence among us.

"Nor do they trouble us with officious fidelity, and useless good will, but take care to earn their livelihood by many meritorious services; they guard our houses, supply our tables with provision, amuse our leisure hours, and discover plots to government.

"The old astronomers denominated stars after their name; and the Egyptians in particular . . . worshipped a dog among the principal of their divinities. The poets represent Diana as spending a great part of her life among a pack of hounds . . . and we know that the illustrious Theseus dedicated much of his time to the same companions. . . . King Charles the Second . . . came always to his council-board accompanied with a favourite spaniel."

Although in eighteenth-century England dogs had increasingly been cherished in the terms of the foregoing "Panegyric upon Dogs," apparently no such succinct and comprehensive tribute to their virtues had yet appeared there. The "Panegyric" served as part of the introduction to Francis Coventry's *The History of Pompey The Little; or, The*

Life and Adventures of a Lap-Dog, first published in London in 1751. Coventry, a Cambridge graduate, dedicated his work to Henry Fielding. It is satirical throughout and aims not so much to delineate Pompey's distinctive behavior or merits as to portray through his sojourns with several varied mistresses the manners, foibles, and social levels of eighteenth-century London life. Thus, in his induction into the home of one "Lady Tempest," Pompey is introduced to his new canine companions: an Italian greyhound, a Dutch pug, two black spaniels of King Charles' breed, a harlequin greyhound, a spotted Dane, and a mouse-colored English bulldog. Among socially aspiring London women, dogs had indeed been liberated from their former servile roles: to assist in the hunt, to guard property, to round up the livestock, or even at times to participate in warfare, as they did under Henry VIII, the Earl of Essex, and Prince Rupert.

The evolution of the dog from its wild state to that of a cherished companion (or even pampered pet) was a long and checkered one. In the nineteenth and twentieth centuries in many countries (including Britain and America) it reached its apogee with a widespread recognition of the dog as a sentient being often with responses on a human level and at times with behavior superior to that of its master or mistress in selfless devotion and compassion, whatever the nature of the canine psychological process or motivation. Moreover, the dog has gained recognition in the aesthetic world as a fit subject for treatment in painting, sculpture, and literature. As Coventry remarked, a definitive treatment of this evolution would require at least a large volume. Some indication of its nature, however, may be suggested by noting first some aspects of canine veneration in mythological, prehistoric, and legendary times and then in five European or Mediterranean cultures between the fourth century B.C. and A.D. 1700. The status of the dog before that time is largely unknown and must be conjectured from the findings of archaeologists and the survival of myths and legends.

The idyllic supposition in Coventry's "Panegyric" that the dog "has ever honoured mankind with his company" has had to yield to more recent historical discoveries. Anthropologists now incline to the view that though dogs and men have inhabited the same territories for incalculable millennia in various parts of the world, evidence indicates that the European domestication of the dog probably occurred some 10,000 years ago; in northern Europe, middens of that era reveal the first presence of both canine and human bones. Previous to that period dogs and men were no doubt rival carnivores seeking animal flesh to sustain their existence. Inasmuch as mankind's superior intelligence provided increasingly effective devices for capture and slaughter, dogs were attracted to human settlements in order to scavenge the remains of the human kill. In effect, dogs and men drifted into a symbiotic understanding whereby men took the choice meats and the dogs helpfully disposed of the offal. Hence the domestication of the dog. Yet since the cultural levels of varied races and areas were, of course, not synchronized, the domestication may have occurred considerably earlier or later than a hundred centuries ago. That among the Incas, for instance, dogs were cherished far beyond mere domestication before 5000 B.C. is indicated by the discovery of two small companion silver statues of a man and a dog estimated to have been made at least by that date.

On the plane of legend, mythology, or religious belief, however, the dog was often venerated and even worshipped in early stages of cultures. Tribes scattered throughout the Far East claimed the dog as an ancestor; and in a myth widely shared among the American Indians a maiden consorts with a dogman and bears his children, whose shaggy coats are gradually eliminated and who gain acceptance into the tribe. In other cultures, especially in the Middle East, dogs such as the three-headed Cerberus of the Greeks and the jackal-headed Anubis of the Egyptians were regarded as beneficent agents in the rituals of death and entrance into the other world. In the Brahminical faith of the Hindus the dog served at times as a guide to the spiritual realm, and in one narrative, as an exemplar of devotion and protection, the dog becomes the divine Dharma.

In western Europe dogs were associated with heroes and could even become saints. In Celtic mythology King Arthur was at times accompanied by his great hound Cabal, whose paw-mark according to local legend may still be seen imprinted in stone in southern Wales. The name of Cuchulain, the legendary Ulster culture hero who had killed the hound of Culann, indicates that he himself had become the watchdog of Culann. And in eastern France near Lyons a French peasant cult paid homage to a greyhound (Guinefort) through the Middle Ages to the nineteenth century by making it a saint. The dog had been killed on the mistaken assumption that it had attacked an infant whereas in reality it had saved the child's life by killing an attacking snake and then, wounded and bloody, had lain down by the cradle as a guardian. Hence the shrine and the long-lived worship of St. Guinefort as the savior of children. This motif of the martyred dog is found in varied versions and with other settings and social levels as early as the Sanskrit in the sixth century B.C. and as late as Mark Twain's more secular and bloodless "A Dog's Tale" at the end of the nineteenth century.

Of all the Eastern Mediterranean cultures of the pre-Christian era, the most devotedly canine was the Egyptian, which honored dogs in both its religion and its art. In paintings and inscriptions they were commemorated over five thousand years ago. They were also honored as guardians of the dead. On one wall of a shrine in Tutankhamun's burial chambers, erected about 3300 years ago, there is an embossed portrait of the king in his chariot accompanied by a hound. At the entrance of another chamber is the recumbent figure of Anubis, the jackal god of the dead, with his canine head and human body. Not only were dogs portrayed in burial chambers as guardians of the dead; they themselves were often embalmed or mummified at death and honored with a period of ceremonial mourning. At Abydos, a necropolis where Anubis reigned, in addition to the tombs of many Pharaohs there was a Catacomb of Dogs where they were both honored and mourned.*

If Homer's *Iliad* can be trusted as a historical record, the pre-Christian veneration of dogs in Egypt was not paralleled in Greece and Troy—at least at the time of their historic war, 1194–1183 B.C. Dogs or allusions to them are omnipresent in the *Iliad* and, though at times they are valued, the predominant image is a pejorative one. They seen as odious scavengers rather than as revered guardians of the dead. Perhaps here originated the widespread contemporary use of the word "dog" as a synonym for baseness or ineptitude or shoddiness—a slightly more genteel condemnation than that implied in the vernacular personal insult, "s.o.b." Yet even this latter epithet the gods and goddesses of the *Iliad* do not hesitate to use: Iris calls Athena "bitch-hearted and shameless," and angry Zeus concludes of Hera that nothing that lives is more "bitch-hearted" than she. It was the Greeks rather than the gods or Trojans, however, who employed "dog" as a term of utmost infamy, and among them the proud and self-infatuated Achilles is the arch dog-hater. Early in the narrative he calls Agamemnon a "covetous cur" who had "the greedy eyes of a dog." When he meets Hector in combat he addresses him as "you dog," and later, when

---

*Some of the comments in the last few pages rely on historical and anthropological data in the National Geographic's *Book of Dogs* or in George and Helen Papashivily's *Dogs and People*.

Hector begs him not to allow his body to be eaten by dogs, Achilles refuses the appeal and again calls him a dog.

It is the war, indeed, that accounts for much of the disparagement of dogs in the *Iliad*. Had it not been for the battlefields full of corpses, the dogs would not have been so conspicuously present in their natural carniverous but repulsive roles. For Greek and Trojan warriors alike the most shameful fate was to have their bodies desecrated by "dogs and carrion birds." Nevertheless, in times of peace and even in war dogs were valued and used by both Greeks and Trojans as caretakers and guardians. Both Priam and Patroclus had "table dogs"—large and handsome household guardians. Yet it was on the farms of the city-states, as Homer repeatedly notes, that the dog was indispensable. He compares the alert Achaeans to dogs who keep "restless watch about a yard full of sheep."

In the *Iliad*, therefore, the ambivalent status of the dog is first fully projected. The ultimately cherished traits of fidelity and companionship scarcely appear in the *Iliad;* but later in the *Odyssey* (in Book XVII) after Odysseus has returned from his wanderings disguised as a beggar and has remained unrecognized by his wife and son, the human-canine relationship reaches a new affective level. The only creature in the household who recognized him was an old flea-bitten dog consigned to the manure pile. On hearing Odysseus' voice he raised his ears and wagged his tail. In turn, Odysseus recognized the dog as Argus, whom he had raised as a pup but had never hunted with because of the Trojan war. When Argus struggled to rise and come to his master, the latter was moved to tears by the realization that after nineteen years Argus still remembered him. Some three millennia later Alexander Pope thought that such fidelity merited commemoration and wrote a sensitive tribute in a brief poem in 1709—several years before he completed his translation of the *Odyssey:*

> When wise Ulysses, from his native coast
> Long kept by wars, and long by tempests tost,
> Arriv'd at last, poor, old, disguis'd, alone,
> To all his friends, and ev'n his Queen unknown;
> Chang'd as he was, with age, and toils, and cares,
> Furrow'd his rev'rend face, and white his hairs,
> In his own palace forc'd to ask his bread,
> Scorn'd by those slaves his former bounty fed,
> Forgot of all his own domestic crew;

The faithful dog alone his rightful master knew!
Unfed, unhous'd, neglected, on the clay,
Like an old servant now cashier'd, he lay;
Touch'd with resentment of ungrateful man,
And longing to behold his ancient Lord again.
Him when he saw—he rose, and crawl'd to meet,
('Twas all he cou'd) and fawn'd, and lick'd his feet,
Seiz'd with dumb joy—then falling by his side,
Own'd his returning Lord, look'd up, and dy'd!*

By the time of the great Athenian cultural flowering in the fifth century B.C., the earlier image of scavenger had evidently faded. Both Socrates and Plato spoke of the estimable traits in canine behavior and intelligence; and later Xenophon, himself a hunting dog breeder and author of the first sportsman's book *Hunting with Dogs,* praised his own dog Horme as possessing the "greatest intelligence and fidelity."

With the founding of the Roman city-state and its absorption of much Greek culture—though it claimed Trojan rather than Greek ancestry—the Athenian view of the dog seems to have been sustained and expanded. Perhaps, too, the Romans were inclined to look kindly on the canine species because of the legend that the infant Romulus, the founder of Rome, and his twin brother, Remus, survived infancy only by being suckled by a wolf. At any rate, by the first century B.C. Cicero had praised dogs for their reliability as guardians and for their fidelity to their masters. A century later Pliny echoed Cicero's praise of canine fidelity and added that it was often displayed to dead masters. He also reported that at one time the Ethiopeans had chosen a dog as their ruler.

On another level the dog in Rome was widely cherished as a pet, possibly on a scale not previously seen in any other society. By the first century A.D. the possession and pampering of small dogs among the well-to-do and powerful families had become virtually epidemic. Romans became especially fond of pet art such as the two small marble greyhounds recently exhibited by the British Museum in London. The museum also contains a tombstone commemorating Margarita, a hunting dog—no doubt one of many such stones in Rome. How strong the bond between dogs and upper-class Romans became is suggested in the twelfth-century Latin *Bestiary* (trans. Terrence H. White, New York,

*"Argus" in Pope's *Poetical Works,* John W. Arden (New York, 1883), pp. 360–361.

1960), which contains the legend of a dog who follows his master, a consul, to prison, brings food to the mouth of the consul after his execution, and swims along the body when it is thrown into the Tiber.

Despite such stories, dogs would have been exposed not only to the perennial cruelty to all animals in all ages but also to the lust of the Roman masses for blood and death in their spectator sports. If the gladiatorial combats and the public assassination of captives and slaves excited the crowds in the Colosseum, it is not to be expected that animals would be exempt. And, indeed, not only in Rome but also in outlying cities such as Pompeii deadly contests between various breeds of carnivorous animals (including dogs) appear on uncovered and restored murals. Found in the ruins of Pompeii was a statue showing a boar being attacked by dogs; but also discovered was the body of a child futilely shielded from the volcanic ash by a dog. Thus lived the dogs of Rome and Pompeii, obliged like all dogs to accept whatever fate men and women allotted them. They were then, as now, adored, respected, tolerated, beaten, starved, and slaughtered in anger or for amusement. The lucky ones happened to have owners as well-meaning and devoted as they.

In the Middle Ages dogs apparently enjoyed a renascent consideration and solicitude, much of it involving unorthodox Christian influences. According to the *Bestiary* no other animal is so perceptive: "He esteems his master highly." The author notes the various breeds and their diverse contributions to mankind's welfare: some track wild creatures; others guard flocks; and house dogs, protecting their master's "palisade," will stand up for their owners "to the death." They will "even guard his body when dead and not leave it." Among the legends cited are those of Jason's dog staying with him at death and dying of starvation, and of King Garamentes' two hundred hounds rescuing him from slavery. Other examples in the *Bestiary* illustrate the sagacity and loyalty of dogs and lead to the assertion that canine behavior is morally instructive and that dogs may be compared to priests in that they counter the influence of the Devil.

In the editorial commentary, T. H. White declares that the Middle Ages were tender toward both dogs and children, and he cites the presence of "dog-boys" at the battle of Agincourt who were provided to stay in the kennels to keep the dogs happy. On the other hand, White brands the uniformly pejorative allusions to dogs in the Bible as callously biased and "revolting." Only Tobias in the Apocrypha, he asserts, gives the dog his due. Indeed, the Christian fathers, with a theological assumption that dogs have no souls, were notably lacking in concern for considerate or humane treatment of animals. This position, in which canine behavior, however courageous or devoted, becomes merely that of automata, was enhanced in the early seventeenth century by the dualistic philosopher Descartes and implicitly echoed not long thereafter by the prolific hymn writer Isaac Watts: "Let dogs delight to bark and bite/For God hath made them so." Yet after Darwin's discoveries placed man in a pattern of evolutionary change, such rigid dualism between man and domesticated animals has faded. Hence in the past two centuries many authors, as selections in *Memorable Dogs* will attest explicitly and implicitly, have rejected or deplored the Cartesian view.

In the Middle Ages, at any rate, when orthodox theology often yielded to the beneficent influence of the Virgin Mary, the dog was fused into Christian art and belief. Thus the Old Testament figure of Judith, who had become a symbol of faith and was linked to the church as the bride of Christ, appears on the north transept portal of Chartres cathedral holding a small dog as a symbol of fidelity. Similarly dogs began to be linked to saints because of their services in times of need —for example, that of the St. Bernards in the snow-covered Alpine passes—and several saints were pictured accompanied by a dog. The order of St. Dominic may have derived its name from the species, for at the saint's birth his mother dreamed that she had given birth to a dog with a torch in his mouth. (The Dominicans may also have been so called from their Latin denomination, Domini canes—i.e., dogs of God.) The Crusaders, too, had dogs in their ranks, and some were fond enough of the species to bring back new breeds from the Middle East to western Europe. Tomb effigies of the Crusaders often included a recumbent dog at their feet. Moreover, in a wider context, dogs appeared on many thirteenth-century coats of arms as well as on the tombs of noble couples who desired a symbolic declaration of their mutual fidelity. Indeed, a thirteenth-century bishop (who may have cared more for symbols than dogs) was buried with a shepherd dog to associate his clerical life with the frequent Biblical image of the shepherd.

Though dogs were acceptable on French cathedral portals and on Crusaders' tombs, they were virtually excluded from English literature of the late Middle Ages. Neither of the two major English writers of the fourteenth century, William Langland or Geoffrey Chaucer, judges them worthy of portrayal or commemoration. Langland's Piers, the Plowman, was of course not a shepherd, but in the long poem *Piers the Plowman* one would expect that the inevitable rural presence of dogs would be reflected in more than two brief phrases of allusion. Though Chaucer's literary range, art, and substance were much more varied than Langland's, the dog finds little place in his poems, tales, and fabliaux. Yet among his Canterbury pilgrims he provides distinctiveness for the Prioress by including her devotion to her "smale houndes." In a modern rendering by J. U. Nicolson:

> She had some little dogs, too, that she fed
> On roasted flesh, or milk and fine white bread,
> But sore she'd weep if one of them were dead,
> Or if men smote it with a rod to smart;
> For pity ruled her, and her tender heart.

In Chaucer's world dogs are apparently cherished only by religious women. Why men smote them is not clear.

The literary indifference to dogs in the late Middle Ages was somewhat altered in the English Renaissance. To be sure, Henry VIII and his daughter Elizabeth loved hunting, of which dogs were an integral part. The hunt, indeed, was the royal sport to such an extent that large tracts of land called "dog tenures" were allotted to those who would keep and care for the monarch's hunting dogs. But the dog's acceptance by royalty under the Tudors ended with the hunt. Hence, when Holbein painted his portrait of Henry VIII no dog was included, although in Europe he had painted such inclusive portraits. At about the same time in southern Europe, Titian and especially Velazquez included dogs in their portraits of royalty, and in the Netherlands Jan van Eyck pictured dogs in family or group scenes. In sixteenth-century England they were virtually excluded, not only from painting but from literature. As Richard Ormond remarked in his volume on the animal painter Sir Edmund Landseer: in "Renaissance literature the image of the dog is invariably used for something base and unclean."

The dog was not so much disparaged in sixteenth-century English literature as, like other domesticated animals such as the horse and cat, merely considered unfit for belletristic levels of treatment. The dominant English literary modes of the time had their particular decorums based in large part on classical and Italian models; the pastoral mode had its characters, forms, and allusions fixed in a love-nature world inherited from Theocritus. Hence it is not surprising that Spenser's

Shepheards Calendar with its twelve monthly eclogues should contain but one brief commonplace reference to dogs. In such longer works as Spenser's *Faerie Queene* given over to religious and political allegory and ethical instruction, the appearance of a typical English dog would have been a serious breach of literary taste. In granting dogs a generous though not distinguished place in the idyllic setting of his long pastoral romance *Arcadia,* Sir Philip Sidney seems chivalrous and courageously unique.

Since Shakespeare's plays may, in Hamlet's phrase, "hold the mirror up to nature" in ways alien to Spenserian modes of poetry, recognizable dogs do appear or are alluded to in several of his works. In *Two Gentlemen of Verona* the clown Launce appears briefly with his dog Crab, whom he describes as the "sourest-natured dog that lives"; and in *A Midsummer Night's Dream* Duke Theseus loves the music of his hounds, which are "bred out of the Spartan kind . . . with ears that sweep away the morning dew." Most memorable of all, however, is King Lear's heart-stricken comment in the first scene of his madness on the heath after he has been cast out by his two older daughters: "The little dogs and all, / Trey, Blanch, and Sweetheart; see, / They bark at me!" Now he must suppose that the legendary fidelity of dogs to their masters is only an ill-founded fable that must yield to the fact that they, too, are self-serving opportunists who truckle to the reigning power. This view seems to have been Shakespeare's, for analyses of Shakespeare's imagery show that his allusions to dogs are consistently derogatory. The spaniel became for him the exemplar of canine fawning.

In the early seventeenth century, however, a historically recorded bond between man and dog clearly revealed that all dogs are not fawning spaniels. It is unfortunate that no appropriate literary tribute has been paid to the most famous dog in English political history. When Prince Rupert, grandson of King James I and nephew of Charles I, was held prisoner in Linz (Austria) for his struggle for what he thought were his father's political rights in Bohemia, he was given a large white dog (probably a poodle) by an English nobleman. The Prince named him "Boy," and during the confinement the two became inseparable companions. When the Prince was released, he returned to England with Boy to support Charles I against the Puritan-Parliamentary antagonists in the English Civil War. Because Boy always accompanied the Prince in his consistently victorious cavalry encounters, the enemy concluded that Boy was a "familiar spirit" with demonic powers—a "four-footed Cavalier" and a "Devil without Doubt," as ironically reported by a contemporary poet, John Cleveland, in a topically obscure poem praising Prince Rupert in 1641. The fear of Boy bred a defamatory pamphlet war against him in which he was pictured as living luxuriously with the royal family and as indulging in abnormal and unseemly conduct. In fact, he was a loyal warrior and devoted companion until his death in the battle of Marston Moor —a casualty which brought rejoicing to the Parliamentarians. (Boy is the subject of an estimable historical novel for juveniles, *Witch-Dog*, by John and Patricia Beatty.)

With the ascendance of the Stuarts to the English throne at the beginning of the seventeenth century, the canine image steadily improved. Indeed, the companionable fondness of the Stuarts for dogs had been dramatically conveyed earlier at the execution of Mary, Queen of Scots, in 1587. As recorded by J. E. Neale in his biography of Queen Elizabeth I: "Mary was accompanied by some of her small dogs. One of them had crept under her clothes; it now [after the beheading] came [out] and lay between her severed head and her shoulders, in her blood." The veracity of the several canine panegyrists (noted in the preceding pages) who had maintained that dogs would be faithful guardians of their masters through and after death had been conspicuously demonstrated by one of Mary's little dogs.

In the 1700s Charles I (as well as his Queen) was devoted to dogs, especially to Prince Rupert's Boy. Moreover, Charles I commissioned Van Dyck to paint a picture of five of his children with their canine companions—a small dog on the floor and a large mastiff in the center forefront with the hand of the young Prince of Wales resting casually on his head. After the Restoration Charles II's palatial living quarters were also the domicile and playground of many of his canine companions, with whom their master spent considerable time. And undoubtedly, as Francis Coventry averred in his "Panegyric," Charles attended his council-board always with a favorite spaniel accompanying him. If dogs could be articulate historians of the fortunes of their species, they would give the highest praise for the royal example of the Stuarts.

The foregoing survey or summary glance at the changing status of the dog during more than five preceding millennia and in several Mediterranean and western European countries is intended to form a background for a clearer perspective on further changes in the past three centuries in Britain and America—the period with which this volume is concerned. The dogs which are presented here have been chosen from several hundred possibilities and do not pretend to form any exclusive or sacrosanct club of memorable dogs.

The dogs in this volume have been found "memorable"—actually remembered by hundreds of twentieth-century readers—because they are appealing and distinctive per se. They also represent the special character and talents of many breeds and frequently the virtues and strength of mongrels. If allotted a whole or a large portion of a book their lives may be seen as heroic and dramatic, and often their virtues are implicitly instructive. Their behavior and fortunes go far in illuminating the character of those who owned them or created them. All who write about them in some measure project themselves and their values even by the diction and style of their writing. Hence the authentic representation of a verbally recorded dog must be completely in the author's words—as it always is in this volume. For this reason many famous dogs that have appeared in comic strips or in films throughout much of this century are omitted. They must be viewed in the comic configurations in which they have been seen or in the film sequences in which their behavior has delighted the eye. Nevertheless the written word is enough to suggest the considerable strengthening during the past three centuries of the ties which in some degree have long formed a canine-human bond.

The selections are arranged chronologically, not so much by date of publication as by the approximate time of the setting.

Memorable Dogs

ALEXANDER POPE'S *Bounce*

■ *Pope's poem acclaiming his dog Bounce, written about 1736, is apparently the first tribute written by any major English author to his own dog. It is a playful denigration of court dogs purportedly written by a country dog, Bounce, who lived at Pope's rural Twickenham, to "sweet Fop," owned by Pope's friend Lady Suffolk. (In this contrast the slightly abridged poem presented here introduces a motif often found in later poems and fiction: the working shepherd dog versus the nobleman's dog in Burns' "Twa Dogs"; the regal estate dog, Buck, in London's* Call of the Wild *versus the sled-dogs of the Klondike, one of whom Buck later becomes; Thurber's fable of the self-assured city dog versus the wiser country dog.) Eschewing the theological controversy over whether dogs have souls, Pope turned his attention to the brutality and needless pain that he knew they suffered. In fact he became a pioneer in seeking more humane treatment for them and other animals, even in the area of vivisection—an endeavor that was carried further by Goldsmith and John Gay. During Pope's last months of illness, Bounce was cared for by Lord Orrery, a friend whom Pope praised for his kindness to animals and "in particular to dogs." The following couplet, which closed a letter Pope wrote to Orrery after the dog's death, was probably the last he wrote: "Ah Bounce! ah gentle Beast! why wouldst thou dye, / When thou had'st Meat enough, and Orrery?"*

BOUNCE to FOP. AN HEROICK EPISTLE
From a DOG at TWICKENHAM To a DOG at Court.

To thee, sweet *Fop,* these Lines I send,
Who, tho' no Spaniel, am a Friend.
Tho, once my Tail in wanton play,
Now frisking this, and then that way,
Chanc'd, with a Touch of just the Tip,
To hurt your Lady-lap-dog-ship;
Yet thence to think I'd bite your Head off!
Sure *Bounce* is one you never read of.

   FOP! you can dance, and make a Leg,
Can fetch and carry, cringe and beg,
And (what's the Top of all your Tricks)
Can stoop to pick up *Strings* and *Sticks.*
We Country Dogs love nobler Sport,
And scorn the Pranks of Dogs at Court. . . .
The worst that Envy, or that Spite
E'er said of me, is, I can bite:
That sturdy Vagrants, Rogues in Rags,
Who poke at me, can make no Brags;
And that to towze such Things as *flutter*
To honest *Bounce* is Bread and Butter.

   While you, and every courtly Fop,
Fawn on the Devil for a Chop,
I've the Humanity to hate
A Butcher, tho' he brings me Meat. . . .

   Your pilf'ring Lord, with simple Pride,
May wear a Pick-lock at his Side;
My Master wants no Key of State,
For *Bounce* can keep his House and Gate.

   When all such Dogs have had their Days,
As knavish *Pams,* and fawning *Trays.* . . .
Fair *Thames* from either ecchoing Shoare
Shall hear, and dread my manly Roar.

See *Bounce*, like *Berecynthia*, crown'd
With thund'ring Offspring all around,
Beneath, beside me, and a top,
A hundred Sons! and not one *Fop*.

Before my Children set your Beef,
Not one true *Bounce* will be a Thief;
Not one without Permission feed,
(Tho' some of *J*——'s hungry Breed)
But whatsoe'er the Father's Race,
From me they suck a little Grace.
While your fine Whelps learn all to steal,
Bred up by Hand on Chick and Veal.

My Eldest-born resides not far,
Where shines great *Strafford's* glittering Star:
My second (Child of Fortune!) waits
At *Burlington's* Palladian Gates:
A third majestically stalks
(Happiest of Dogs!) in *Cobham's* Walks:
One ushers Friends to *Bathurst's* Door;
One fawns, at *Oxford's*, on the Poor.

Nobles, whom Arms or Arts adorn,
Wait for my Infants yet unborn.
None but a Peer of Wit and Grace,
Can hope a Puppy of my Race.

And O! wou'd Fate the Bliss decree
To mine (a Bliss too great for me)
That two, my tallest Sons, might grace
Attending each with stately Pace,
Iülus' [Prince of Wales'] Side, as erst *Evander's*,
To keep off Flatt'rers, Spies, and Panders,
To let no noble Slave come near,
And scare Lord *Fannys* from his Ear:
Then might a Royal Youth, and true,
Enjoy at least a Friend—or two:
A Treasure, which, of Royal kind,
Few but Himself deserve to find.

Then *Bounce* ('tis all that *Bounce* can crave)
Shall wag her Tail within the Grave.

And tho' no Doctors, Whig or Tory ones,
Except the Sect of *Pythagoreans*,
Have Immortality assign'd
To any Beast, but *Dryden's* Hind:
Yet Master *Pope,* whom Truth and Sense
Shall call their Friend some Ages hence,
Tho' now on loftier Themes he sings
Than to bestow a Word on *Kings,*
Has sworn by *Sticks* (the Poet's Oath,
And Dread of Dogs and Poets both)
Man and his Works he'll soon renounce,
And roar in Numbers worthy *Bounce.*

JOHN GAY'S *Shock*

■ *Much of eighteenth-century literature involving dogs was a satiric attack on women's excessive attachment to the species; but John Gay, famed for his* Beggar's Opera, *gave a gentler mock-heroic treatment to Celia and her Shock. He was fond of dogs and wrote much about them in* Rural Sports. *Like Pope and Goldsmith, he consistently deplored cruelty to animals.*

AN ELEGY ON A LAP-DOG

SHOCK'S fate I mourn; poor Shock is now no more,
Ye Muses mourn, ye chamber-maids deplore.
Unhappy Shock! yet more unhappy Fair,
Doom'd to survive thy joy and only care!
Thy wretched fingers now no more shall deck,
And tie the fav'rite ribband round his neck;
No more thy hand shall smooth his glossy hair,
And comb the wavings of his pendent ear.
Yet cease thy flowing grief, forsaken maid;
All mortal pleasures in a moment fade:
Our surest hope is in an hour destroy'd,
And love, best gift of heav'n, not long enjoy'd.

Methinks I see her frantic with despair,
Her streaming eyes, wrung hands, and flowing hair;
Her Mechlen pinners rent the floor bestrow,
And her torn fan gives real signs of woe.
Hence Superstition, that tormenting guest,
That haunts with fancied fears the coward breast;
No dread events upon this fate attend,
Stream eyes no more, no more thy tresses rend.
Tho' certain omens oft forewarn a state,
And dying lions show the monarch's fate;
Why should such fears bid Celia's sorrow rise;
For when a Lap-dog falls no lover dies.

Cease, Celia, cease; restrain thy flowing tears,
Some warmer passion will dispel thy cares.
In man you'll find a more substantial bliss,
More grateful toying and a sweeter kiss.

He's dead. Oh lay him gently in the ground!
And may his tomb be by this verse renown'd.
Here Shock, the pride of all his kind, is laid;
Who fawn'd like man, but ne'er like man betray'd.

OLIVER GOLDSMITH'S *Mad Dog*

■ *This well-known humorously ironic poem was the outgrowth of what Goldsmith deplored in his* Citizen of the World *as an epidemic hysteria about mad dogs in England in the early 1760s. The mayor of London, for instance, ordered all loose dogs on the streets to be killed; and irresponsible rumors of fatal bites were so rife that thousands of innocent dogs were needlessly harassed and slain. Goldsmith estimated that not more than three or four persons a year suffered rabid bites. The "Elegy" was not published until 1766, when it appeared in Goldsmith's* The Vicar of Wakefield, *sung with guitar accompaniment by the Vicar's youngest son, Bill.*

AN ELEGY ON THE DEATH OF A MAD DOG

Good people all, of every sort,
    Give ear unto my song;
And if you find it wond'rous short,
    It cannot hold you long.

In Isling town there was a man,
    Of whom the world might say,
That still a godly race he ran,
    Whene'er he went to pray.

A kind and gentle heart he had,
    To comfort friends and foes;
The naked every day he clad,
    When he put on his cloaths.

And in that town a dog was found,
    As many dogs there be,
Both mongrel, puppy, whelp, and hound,
    And curs of low degree.

This dog and man at first were friends;
    But when a pique began,
The dog, to gain some private ends,
    Went mad and bit the man.

Around from all the neighbouring streets,
    The wondering neighbors ran,
And swore the dog had lost his wits,
    To bite so good a man.

The wound it seem'd both sore and sad,
    To every christian eye;
And while they swore the dog was mad,
    They swore the man would die.

But soon a wonder came to light,
    That shew'd the rogues they lied,
The man recovered of the bite,
    The dog it was that dy'd.

■ *Although Cowper during much of his life felt himself "hunted by spiritual hounds," there were periods when he wrote light verse and cherished the companionship of his dog Beau. Gracefully he recognizes the logic of Beau's defense of his canine delinquincy; and in another poem, "The Dog and the Water Lily" (based on an actual event), he recognizes Beau's superior skill in gathering lilies. Understandably, in 1789 when Beau followed a neighbor's dog home, Cowper wrote that he "could by no means spare my dog."*

ON A SPANIEL,
CALLED BEAU,
KILLING A YOUNG BIRD

A spaniel, Beau, that fares like you,
    Well fed, and at his ease,
Should wiser be than to pursue
    Each trifle that he sees.

But you have kill'd a tiny bird
    Which flew not till to-day,
Against my orders, whom you heard
    Forbidding you the prey.

Nor did you kill that you might eat,
　　And ease a doggish pain,
For him, though chased with furious heat,
　　You left where he was slain.

Nor was he of the thievish sort,
　　Or one whom blood allures,
But innocent was all his sport
　　Whom you have torn for yours.

My dog! what remedy remains,
　　Since, teach you all I can,
I see you, after all my pains,
　　So much resemble man!

BEAU'S REPLY

Sir, when I flew to seize the bird
　　In spite of your command,
A louder voice than yours I heard,
　　And harder to withstand.

You cried—forbear!—but in my breast
　　A mightier cried—proceed!—
'Twas Nature, sir, whose strong behest
　　Impelled me to the deed.

Yet much as nature I respect,
　　I ventured once to break
(As you perhaps may recollect)
　　Her precept for your sake;

And when your linnet on a day,
　　Passing his prison door,
Had flutter'd all his strength away,
　　And panting press'd the floor;

Well knowing him a sacred thing,
      Not destined to my tooth,
I only kiss'd his ruffled wing,
      And lick'd the feathers smooth.

Let my obedience then excuse
      My disobedience now,
Nor some reproof yourself refuse
      From your aggrieved bow-wow;

If killing birds be such a crime
      (Which I can hardly see),
What think you, sir, of killing time
      With verse address'd to me?

JAMES FENIMORE COOPER'S *Hector*

■ *Hector appears earlier in* The Pioneers *(1823), the first of Cooper's five novels which deal with freedom-loving frontiersman Natty Bumppo (alias Leatherstocking). The setting is western New York in 1793, when the first settlements and the beginning of an ordered society impinge on aging Leatherstocking's freedom as a woodsman and hunter. Hector is described there as "old," yet with a "bay" which could be distinguished "among ten thousand." In* The Prairie *(1827) dog and master continue their search for freedom in the open prairies of the West where both die under the care of friendly Pawnees. Reared under Moravian influence, Leatherstocking assumed that Hector had no soul or afterlife but paid him a memorable tribute after his death by asking to be buried at his side.*

From THE PRAIRIE

The sun had fallen below the crest of the nearest wave of the prairie. In the centre of this flood of fiery light a human form appeared. The figure was colossal; the attitude musing and melancholy. In the mean-time a grey and more sober light had succeeded, and the proportions of the fanciful form became less exaggerated. Not withstanding his years, there was that about this solitary being which said that time had laid his hand heavily upon him. As the party [of the Ishmael Bush family of emigrants from Kentucky] drew nigher to this solitary being, a low growl issued from the grass at his feet, and then a tall, gaunt, toothless hound arose lazily from his lair. "Down, Hector, down," said his master. "What have ye to do, pup, with men who journey on their lawful callings?" . . .

The trapper loitered about the place [the emigrants' encampment], and then he slowly retired from the spot into the waste. At length he came to a stand; he stood lost in deep contemplation for several minutes, during which time his hound came and crouched at his feet. A deep, menacing growl from the faithful animal first aroused him from his musing. "What now, dog?" he said, as if he addressed a being of an intelligence equal to his own, and speaking in a voice of great affection. "What is it, pup? ha! Hector; what is it nosing, now? It won't do, dog; it won't do; the very fa'ns [fawns] play in open view of us, without minding so worn out curs, as you and I. Instinct is their gift, Hector; and they have found out how little we are to be feared." The dog responded to the words by a long and plaintive whine, as if he held an intelligent communication with one who so well knew how to interpret dumb discourse. "This is a manifest warning, Hector!" the trapper continued. "What is it, pup; speak plainer, dog; what is it?" The hound had already laid his nose to the earth. But the keen, quick glances of his master soon caught a glimpse of a distant figure. "Come nigher; we are friends," said the trapper, associating himself with his companion by long use; "none will harm you." The old man turned towards her [Ellen Wade, niece of Ishmael Bush] with a look of kindness and interest. "Hush, Hector, hush," he added, in reply to a low growl from his hound. "The dog scents mischief in the wind!" The girl raised her eyes; but she rather manifested impatience than alarm. A short bark from the dog, however, soon gave a new direction to the looks of both.

"Call in your dog," said a firm, deep, manly voice; "I love a hound, and should be sorry to do an injury to the animal." "You hear what is said about you, pup?" the trapper answered; "come hither, fool. His growl and his bark are all that is left him now; you may come on, friend; the hound is toothless." The stranger [Paul Hover, the bee-hunter] sprang eagerly forward. "Tell me, lad; did you ever strike a leaping buck atwixt the antlers? Hector; quiet, pup; quiet. The very name of venison quickens the blood of the cur." The trapper drew slowly aside, completely out of ear shot of the hurried dialogue that instantly commenced between the two he had left. He was accompanied by his indolent but attached dog, who once more made his bed at the feet of his master.

The dog, who had manifested such a propensity to sleep, now arose and looked abroad into the prairie. Then, seemingly content with his examination, he returned to his comfortable post. "What; again Hector!" said the trapper; "tell it all to his master, pup; what is it?" Hector answered with another growl. After a short pause [Leatherstocking] whistled the dog to his side, and turning to his [rejoined] companions, said, "I will not take upon myself to say what mischief is brewing, nor will I vouch that even the hound himself knows so much; but, that evil is nigh I have heard from the mouth of one who never lies. I did think that your presence made him uneasy; but his nose has been on a long scent the whole evening." The youth and his female companion [Paul and Ellen] had made hurried conjectures when a current of night air brought the rush of trampling footsteps too sensibly to their ears to render mistake any longer possible. "Down, down into the grass," whispered the trapper. The trapper, who had called in his hound, kneeled in the cover also, and kept a watchful eye on the band [of Indians]. . . .

"Cut more into the heart of it, lad" said the trapper, who had served the bee-hunter the banquet [of bison's hump]. "Here, Hector," tossing the patient hound a portion of the meat, "you have need of strength, my friend, in your old days as well as your master. Now, lad, there is a dog that has eaten and slept wiser and better, ay, and that of richer food, than any king of them all! and why? because he has used and not abused the gifts of his Maker. He was made a hound, and like a hound has he feasted. Them did He create men; but they have eaten like famished wolves. A good and prudent dog has Hector proved, and never have I found one of his breed false in nose or friendship." . . .

"Follow *me!*" echoed Esther [Bush, Ishmael's wife]. "Who so proper as a mother, to head a search for her own lost child?" Another half-hour passed. "Hold!" cried Ishmael, "we have hunters nigh." He was still speaking, when the animals in question came leaping on the track of the deer. One was an aged dog [Hector], and the other a pup; and in another minute they would have been running open-mouthed with the deer in view, had not the younger dog suddenly bounded from the course, and uttered a cry of surprise. His aged companion stopped also, and returned panting to the place where the other was whirling around in mad evolutions. But the elder hound seated himself and raised a long, loud, and wailing howl. "Come away, boys; leave the hounds to sing their tunes," Ishmael said. "Come *not* away!" cried Esther.

"There is a meaning and a warning in this." Above the little brake, the flocks of birds held their flight, circling about the spot, and making bold swoops upon the thicket. "Call in the dogs!" [Esther] said, "and put them into the thicket." But the elder dog was restrained by some extraordinary sensation. After proceeding a few yards, he stood trembling in all his aged limbs. "Have I a man among my children?" demanded Esther. Preparing their arms with utmost care, they [Bush's sons, Abner and Enoch] advanced to the brake. Then arose two loud and piercing cries. "Come back, my children!" cried the woman. But her voice was hushed as the two adventurers re-appeared, pale, and nearly insensible, and laid at her feet the stiff and motionless body of the lost [son] Asa. The dogs uttered a long and closing howl, and then disappeared on the forsaken trail of the deer. . . .

The trapper turned away from his warm-hearted companion [Paul] and having called Hector from the boat, he seemed anxious to utter a few words more. "Captain [Middleton]," he resumed, "there is one thing I will say, and that is not so much on my own behalf as on that of another person. Here is Hector, a good and faithful pup, that has long outlived the time of a dog. But the creatur' has his feelings as well as a Christian. He has consorted latterly with his kinsman, there, in such a sort as to find great pleasure in his company, and it touches my feelings to part the pair so soon. If you will set a value on your hound, I will endeavor to send it to you in the spring. Or, I will just ask you for his loan through the winter. I think my pup will not last beyond that time." "Take him, take him," cried Middleton; "take anything!" The old man whistled the younger dog to the land; and then proceeded to the final adieux. He was last seen standing on the low point with Hector crouched at his feet, and the younger dog frisking along the sands.

In the autumn of the year, the young man [Middleton] found himself not far from the Pawnee towns. He determined to cross the country and to inquire into the fate of his friend the trapper. At length the cavalcade, at whose head rode Middleton and Paul, descended to the village of the Loups [Pawnees]. A group of horsemen were at length seen advancing toward them, slow and dignified. When they entered the town, its inhabitants were seen collected in an open space. The trapper was placed on a rude seat made to support his frame in an easy attitude. Between his feet lay the figure of a hound, with its head crouching to the earth, and so perfectly easy and natural was its position, that a second glance was necessary to tell Middleton he saw only the skin of Hector, stuffed, by Indian tenderness and ingenuity, to represent the living animal. When he had placed his guests in front of the dying man, Hard-Heart [the Pawnee chief], after a pause, demanded—"Does my father hear the words of his son?" "Speak," returned the trapper, "I shortly shall be beyond the reach of your voice. I fear I have not altogether followed the gifts of my color, as I find it a little painful to give up the use of the rifle, and the comforts of the chase. Ay, Hector," he continued leaning forward a little, and feeling for the ears of the hound, "our parting has come at last, dog, and it will be a long hunt. You have been an honest, and a bold, and a faithful hound. Pawnee, you cannot slay the pup on my grave, for where a Christian dog falls there he lies forever; but you can be kind to him after I am gone, for the love you bear his master."

"The words of my father are in my ears," returned the young partisan. "Do you hear what the chief has promised, dog?" demanded the trapper. Receiving no answering look nor hearing any friendly whine, the old man felt for the mouth, and endeavored to force his hand between the cold lips. The truth then flashed upon him. Falling back in his seat, he hung his head, like one who felt a severe shock. "The dog is dead!" muttered the trapper, after a pause of many minutes; "a hound has his time as well a man; and well has he filled his days! Captain," he added, "I am glad you have come, for though kind, these Indians are not the men to lay the head of a white man in his grave. I have been thinking, too, of this dog at my feet; it will not do to set forth the opinion that a Christian can expect to meet his hound again; still there can be little harm in placing what is left of so faithful a servant nigh the bones of his master." "It shall be as you desire," [said Middleton]. "I'm glad you think with me in this matter. In order, then to save labor, lay the pup at my feet; or for that matter, put him side by side. A hunter need never be ashamed to be found in company with his dog!"

THOMAS CAMPBELL'S *Tray*

■ *With the publication of* The Pleasures of Hope *in 1799, young Thomas Campbell was suddenly vaulted from depression and obscurity to national acclaim by his Scottish countrymen, who were inspired by the volume's hortative emphasis and charmed by its mellifluous verse. Because Campbell's life had had its own anxieties and despair, he could all the more convincingly convey the value of and need for hope by also portraying the plight of some of those who had been deprived of it. The most memorable of those portraits has proved to be that of the harper and his dog Tray.*

THE HARPER

On the green banks of Shannon, when Sheelah was nigh,
No blithe Irish lad was so happy as I;
No harp like my own could so cheerily play,
And wherever I went was my poor dog Tray.

When at last I was forced from my Sheelah to part,
She said—while the sorrow was big at her heart—
"Oh! remember your Sheelah, when far, far away;
And be kind, my dear Pat, to our poor dog Tray."

Poor dog! he was faithful and kind to be sure,
And he constantly loved me, although I was poor;
When the sour-looking folks sent me heartless away,
I had always a friend in my poor dog Tray.

When the road was so dark, and the night was so cold,
And Pat and his dog were grown weary and old,
How snugly we slept in my old coat of grey,
And he licked me for kindness—my poor dog Tray.

Though my wallet was scant, I remembered his case,
Nor refused my last crust to his pitiful face;
But he died at my feet on a cold winter day,
And I played a sad lament for my poor dog Tray.

Where now shall I go, poor, forsaken, and blind?
Can I find one to guide me, so faithful and kind?
To my sweet native village, so far, far away,
I can never more return with my poor dog Tray.

WILLIAM WORDSWORTH'S *Music*

AND *Dog*

■ *Music was a dog Wordsworth knew well for she belonged to Mrs. Wordsworth's brother. Wordsworth wrote a second poem about Music after her death, but it adds little to her characterization. A more memorable poem the same year (1805) was "Fidelity," which marveled at a dog that had kept lonely vigil for three months over the body of its master who had fallen to his death from Mount Helvellyn. This instance of canine devotion was also commemorated in a poem by Sir Walter Scott and a painting by Sir Edwin Landseer.*

INCIDENT, CHARACTERISTIC OF A FAVORITE DOG

On his morning rounds the Master
Goes to learn how all things fare;
Searches pasture after pasture,
Sheep and cattle eyes with care;
And, for silence or for talk,
He hath comrades in his walk;
Four dogs, each pair of different breed,
Distinguished two for scent, and two for speed.

See a hare before him started!
—Off they fly in earnest chase;

Every dog is eager-hearted,
All the four are in the race:
And the hare whom they pursue
Knows from instinct what to do;
Her hope is near: no turn she makes;
But, like an arrow, to the river takes.

Deep the river was and crusted
Thinly by a one night's frost;
But the nimble Hare hath trusted
To the ice, and safely crost;
She hath crost, and without heed
All are following at full speed,
When, lo! the ice, so thinly spread,
Breaks—and the greyhound, DART is over-head!

Better fate have PRINCE and SWALLOW—
See them cleaving to the sport!
MUSIC hath no heart to follow,
Little MUSIC, she stops short.
She hath neither wish nor heart,
Hers is now another part:
A loving creature she, and brave!
And fondly strives her struggling friend to save.

From the brink her paws she stretches,
Very hands as you would say!
And afflicting moans she fetches,
As he breaks the ice away.
For herself she hath no fears,—
Him alone she sees and hears,—
Makes efforts with complainings; nor gives o'er
Until her fellow sinks to re-appear no more.

FIDELITY

A BARKING sound the Shepherd hears,
A cry as of a dog or fox;
He halts—and searches with his eyes
Among the scattered rocks:
And now at distance can discern
A stirring in a brake of fern;
And instantly a dog is seen,
Glancing through that covert green.

The Dog is not of mountain breed;
Its motions, too, are wild and shy;
With something, as the Shepherd thinks,
Unusual in its cry:
Nor is there anyone in sight
All round, in hollow or on height;
Nor shout, nor whistle strikes his ear;
What is the creature doing here?

It was a cove, a huge recess,
That keeps, till June, December's snow;
A lofty precipice in front,
A silent tarn below!
Far in the bosom of Helvellyn,
Remote from public road or dwelling,
Pathway, or cultivated land;
From trace of human foot or hand.

There sometimes doth a leaping fish
Send through the tarn a lonely cheer;
The crags repeat the raven's croak,
In symphony austere;
Thither the rainbow comes—the cloud—
And mists that spread the flying shroud;
And sunbeams; and the sounding blast,
That, if it could, would hurry past;
But that enormous barrier holds it fast.

Not free from boding thoughts, a while
The Shepherd stood; then makes his way
O'er rocks and stones, following the Dog
As quickly as he may;
Nor far had gone before he found
A human skeleton on the ground;
The appalled Discoverer with a sigh
Looks round, to learn the history.

From those abrupt and perilous rocks
The Man had fallen, that place of fear!
At length upon the Shepherd's mind
It breaks, and all is clear:
He instantly recalled the name,
And who he was, and whence he came;
Remembered, too, the very day
On which the Traveller passed this way.

But hear a wonder, for whose sake
This lamentable tale I tell!
A lasting monument of words
This wonder merits well.
The Dog, which still was hovering nigh,
Repeating the same timid cry,
This Dog, had been through three months' space
A dweller in that savage place.

Yes, proof was plain that, since the day
When this ill-fated Traveller died,
The Dog had watched about the spot,
Or by his master's side:
How nourished here through such long time
He knows who gave that love sublime;
And gave that strength of feeling, great
Above all human estimate!

SIR WALTER SCOTT'S *Camp*

■ *Although Scott was so fond of dogs that he had many, Camp was undoubtedly his favorite. His portrait was painted with Camp included, and his own verbal portraits of Camp's qualities reflect the nature of his pleasure in canine companionship. The doors of the room in which he wrote his novels were always open to his dogs; indeed, he remarked that he never sat down to write without a dog at his side. They appear prominently in several of his novels, and, like Wordsworth, Scott wrote a poem ("Helvellyn") to commemorate the long vigil kept by a dog over "the much-loved remains of her master," who had fallen to his death from the mountain.*

To Dr. Leyden

5 JULY 1806

Camp is as much in favor, as stout and hearty as ever. He had a very violent illness about a year ago, which had like to have carried him off. He was unable to stir for about two days, and eat nothing but some milk, which I forced into his mouth with a teaspoon; but by dint of using that noble remedy *un petit lavement,* frequently repeated, we brought on a crisis, and his health was restored, to the general joy of the family.

To Lady Abercorn

Two of the enclosed were sent me yesterday and I take the liberty to beg your acceptance of one of them. It [Raeburn's portrait of Scott, including Camp] is prettily engraved and not worth refusing. The dog is my poor deceased *Camp*, whom your Ladyship has often heard me mention: my friends wrote as many elegies for him in different languages as ever were poured forth by Oxford or Cambridge on the death of a crowned head. I have Latin, French, Italian, Greek, Hebrew, German, Arabic, and Hindostanee poems to his memory.

To Mr. Stevenson, Edinburgh bookseller,
with Howe's painting of Camp

Camp was got by a black and tan English terrier . . . out of a thoroughbred English brindled bull-bitch. . . . He was of great strength and very handsome, extremely sagacious, faithful and affectionate to the human species, and possessed of a great turn for gayety and drollery. Although he was never taught any tricks, he learned some of his own accord, and understood whatever was said to him as well as any creature I ever saw. His great fault was an excessive ferocity towards his own species, which sometimes brought his Master and himself into dangerous scrapes. He used to accompany me always in coursing, of which he was a great amateur, and was one of the best dogs for finding hares I ever saw, though I have since had very fine terriers. At last he met with an accident which gave him a sprain in the back from which he never recovered, after which he could not follow when I went out on horseback. The servant used to tell him when I was seen coming home. I lived then at Ashestiel, and there were two ways by which I might return. If the servant said, "Camp, your Master is coming back by the hill," he ran to meet me in that direction. If the lad said, "by the ford," he came down to the bank of the river to welcome me; nor did he ever make a mistake in the direction named. I might mention many instances of similar sagacity. He was seldom scolded or punished, and except in his pugnacious propensities, I never saw so manageable a dog. I could even keep him from fighting so long as I had my eye on him, but if I quitted my vigilance for a moment, he was sure to worry the dog nearest to him.

He is painted in two portraits of his owner by Raeburn. . . . He lived till about twelve years old, and might have lived longer but for the severe exercises he had taken when young, and a considerable disposition to voracity, especially where animal food was to be come by. I could add a number of curious anecdotes of his sagacity, but they are connected with a family loss. . . . There is enough to illustrate Mr. Stevenson's picture, which was painted by Mr. Howe, then a painter of animals of some merit.

From MEMOIRS OF THE LIFE OF SIR WALTER SCOTT

He [Camp] died about January, 1809, and was buried in a fine moonlight night, in the little garden behind the house in Castle Street, immediately opposite to the window at which Scott usually sat writing. My wife [Scott's daughter] tells me she remembers the whole family standing in tears about the grave, as her father himself smoothed down the turf above Camp with the saddest expression of face she had ever seen in him. He had been engaged to dine abroad that day, but apologized on account of "the death of a dear old friend."

LORD BYRON'S *Boatswain*

■ *In the instability of his own life in what he thought to be an endemic hypocrisy and injustice in English society, Byron found a venerable antithesis in the abiding fidelity of his dog, Boatswain. Byron wrote to his friend Hodgson that "Boatswain . . . expired in a state of madness . . . after suffering much, yet retaining all the gentleness of his nature to the last." He was buried in the garden of Newstead Abbey in a tomb intended for Byron. In two different wills, Byron included his wish to be buried beside Boatswain, omitting it from later ones only after making the decision to sell Newstead. Almost a decade after Boatswain's death the dog remained for him the emblem of fidelity. In the dream poem "Darkness" (1816) as social anarchy follows the sudden disappearance of all cosmic light, he finds one dog who "was faithful to a corse [sic], and kept / The birds and beasts and famished men at bay," and "licking the hand / Which answered not with a caress—he died."*

EPITAPH TO A NEWFOUNDLAND DOG
(Inscription on Boatswain's Tomb)

> Near this spot
> Are deposited the Remains of one
> Who possessed Beauty without Vanity,
> Strength without Insolence,
> Courage without Ferocity,
> And all the virtues of Man, without his Vices.

This Praise, which would be unmeaning Flattery
If inscribed over human ashes
Is but a just tribute to the Memory of
Boatswain, a Dog,
Who was born at Newfoundland, May, 1803,
And died at Newstead Abbey, Nov. 18, 1808.

INSCRIPTION ON THE MONUMENT
OF A NEWFOUNDLAND DOG

When some proud son of man returns to earth,
Unknown to glory, but upheld by birth,
The sculptor's art exhausts the pomp of woe,
And storied urns record who rests below;
When all is done, upon the tomb is seen,
Not what he was, but what he should have been:
But the poor dog, in life the firmest friend,
The first to welcome, foremost to defend,
Whose honest heart is still his master's own,
Who labors, fights, lives, breathes for him alone,
Unhonor'd falls, unnoticed all his worth,
Denied in heaven the soul he held on earth;
While man, vain insect! hopes to be forgiven,
And claims himself a sole exclusive heaven.
Oh man! Thou feeble tenant of an hour,
Debased by slavery, or corrupt by power,
Who knows thee well must quit thee with disgust,
Degraded mass of animated dust!
Thy love is lust, thy friendship all a cheat,
Thy smiles hypocrisy, thy words deceit!
By nature vile, ennobled but by name,
Each kindred brute might bid thee blush for shame.
Ye! who perchance behold this simple urn,
Pass on—it honors none you wish to mourn:
To mark a friend's remains these stones arise;
I never knew but one,—and here he lies.

Newstead Abbey, November 30, 1808

JOHN CLARE'S *Shepherd's Dog*

■ *Probably no other working dog in American or British literature has been so fully and precisely observed as the shepherd's dog described by John Clare, the "Northhamptonshire peasant poet," a century and a half ago. In the dog's relationship with his master, in his sense of being one of the shepherd's family, and in his sense of responsibility, he is typical of thousands of dogs on small farms in Britain and America of the past two centuries. Undoubtedly the lucid realism of the portrayal was rooted in Clare's provincial life as farmer and shepherd; but unfortunately he became a vagrant and spent the last portion of his life in an asylum. The uniqueness and validity of this portrayal make this poem a treasure for those who know and love dogs.*

From THE SHEPHERD'S CALENDAR

January

The shepherd seeks his cottage warm
And tucks his hook beneath his arm. . . .
His dog wi [with] swifter pace proceeds
And barks to urge his masters speed
Then turns and looks him in the face
And trotts before wi mending pace
Till out of whistle from the swain

He sits him down and barks again
Anxious to greet the opend door
And meet the cottage fire once more. . . .
The shepherd from his labour free
Dancing his childern on his knee
While underneath his masters seat
The tird dog lies in slumbers sweet
Startling and whimpering in his sleep
Chasing still the straying sheep. . . .

February

The barking dogs by lane and wood
Drive sheep afield from foddering ground . . .
Nor more behind his masters heels
The dog creeps oer his winter pace
But cocks his tail and oer the fields
Runs many a wild and random chase
Following in spite of chiding calls
The startld cat wi harmless glee
Scaring her up the weed green walls
Or mossy mottld apple tree
As crows from morning perches flye
He barks and follows them in vain
Een larks will catch his nimble eye
And off he starts and barks again
Wi breathless haste and blinded guess
Oft following where the hare hath gone
Forgetting in his joys excess
His frolic puppy days are done

July

Along the roads in passing crowds . . .
Scotch droves of beast a little breed
In swelterd weary mood proceed . . .
At whom the shepherds dog will rise
And shake himself and in supprise
Draw back and waffle in affright
Barking the traveller out of sight. . . .

The shepherd startles from his bed . . .
Again his journey he pursues
Lengthening his track along the dews
And his dog that turnd to pick
From his sides the sucking tick . . .
Pricks up his ears to see twas gone
And shakes his hide and hastens on . . .
And oft amid the sunny day
Will join a partner in his play
And in his antic tricks and glee
Will prove as fond of sport as he
And by the flag pool summer warm
He'll watch the motions of his arm
That holds a stick or stone to throw
In the sun gilded flood below
And head oer ears he danses in
Nor fears to wet his curly skin
The [herding] boys field cudgel to restore
And brings it in his mouth ashore
And eager as for crust or bone
He'll run to catch the pelted stone
Till wearied out he shakes his hide
And drops his tail and sneaks aside
Unheeding whistles shouts and calls
To take a rest where thickly falls
The rush clumps shadows there [where] he lyes
Licking his skin and catching flyes
Or picking tween his stretching feet
The bone he had not time to eat. . . .
The shepherd long wi heat opprest
Betakes him to his cottage rest
And his tird dog that plods along
Wi panting breath and lolling tongue
Runs eager as the brook appears
And dashes in head over ears . . .
Lapping while he floats about
To quench his thirst then drabbles out
And shakes his coat and like the swain
Is happy night is come again. . . .

August

When the sun stoops to meet the Western sky
And noons hot hours have wanderd weary bye . . .
So dog forgoes his sleep awhile or play
Springing at frogs that rustling jump away
To watch each morsel that the boon bestows
And wait the bone or crumb the shepherd throws
For shepherds are no more of ease possest
But share the harvests labours with the rest

September

The dog beside the threshold lyes
Mocking sleep with half shut eyes
With head crouched down upon his feet
Till strangers pass his sunny seat
Then quick he pricks his ears to hark
And bustles up to growl and bark
While boys in fear stop short their song
And sneak on hurrys fears along
And beggar creeping like a snail
To make his hungry hopes prevail
Oer the warm heart of charity
Leaves his lame halt and hastens bye

November

Gaunt greyhounds now their coursing sports impart
Wi long legs stretchd on tip toe for the chase
And short loose ear and eye upon the start
Swift as the wind their motions they unlace
When bobs the hare up from her hiding place
Who in its furry coat of fallow stain
Squats on the lands or wi a dodging pace
Tryes its old coverts of wood grass to gain
And oft by cunning ways makes all their speed in vain.

CHARLES LAMB'S *Dash*

■ *Even the style as well as the substance of Lamb's jocular letter to Patmore suggests the erratic character of Dash. Patmore described him as "tempestuous," "tyrannical," and, indeed, "mad." Probably because of his disposition, Dash's life was a mobile existence among several of Lamb's friends, including the poet Thomas Hood, who first owned him, Patmore, and Edward Moxon. At least his antics provided material for Lamb's humor.*

To Peter George Patmore

JUNE 1827

Excuse my anxiety—but how is Dash? . . . Goes he muzzled, or *aperto ore*? Are his intellects sound, or does he wander a little in *his* conversation? You cannot be too careful to watch the first symptoms of incoherence. The first illogical snarl he makes, to St. Luke's with him! All the dogs here are going mad, if you believe the overseers; but I protest they seem to me very rational and collected. But nothing is so deceitful as mad people to those who are not used to them. Try him with hot water. If he won't lick it up, it is a sign he does not like it. Does his tail wag horizontally or perpendicularly? That has decided the fate of many dogs in Enfield. Is his general deportment cheerful? I mean when he is pleased—for otherwise there is no judging. You can't be too careful. Has he bit any of the children yet? If he has, have them shot, and keep *him* for curiosity, to see if it was the hydrophobia. . . . Do you get paunch for him? Take care the sheep was sane. You might pull out his teeth (if he would let you), and then you need not mind if he were as mad as a Bedlamite. It would be rather fun to see his odd ways. . . . He'd be like a Fool kept in the family, to keep the household in good humour with their own understanding. You might teach him the mad dance set to the mad howl. . . .

If the slightest suspicion arises in your breast, that all is not right with him [Dash], muzzle him, and lead him in a string . . . to Hood's, his quondam master, and he'll take him in at any time. You may mention your suspicion or not, as you like, or as you think it may wound or not Mr. H's feelings. Hood, I know, will wink at a few follies in Dash, in consideration of his former sense. Besides, Hood is deaf, and if you hinted anything, ten to one he would not hear you. . . . I send my love in a———to Dash.

To Peter George Patmore

JULY 19, 1827

Dash is frightful this morning, he whines and stands up on his hind legs, he misses Becky [Lamb's servant], who is gone to town. I took him to Barnet the other day, and he couldn't eat his victuals after it. Pray God his intellectuals be not slipping. . . . Give both our Loves ("all three," says dash) to Mrs. Patmore. . . .

Bull's-eye

■ *Although Dickens apparently did not have Scott's fond and personal association with dogs, he was convincingly knowledgeable about the details and patterns of their behavior. In a half-dozen of his novels they play a notable part, especially in mirroring the essential character of their owners. Dora's Jip in* David Copperfield *and Sikes' Bull's-eye in* Oliver Twist *are the most memorably characterized and become an integral part of each novel's development. Bull's-eye is distinctively interesting because of the mixed responses of loyalty and fear with which he responds to his intemperate and ruthless master. Like several other of Dickens' fictional dogs, he dies loyally at the time of his owner's death.*

From OLIVER TWIST

"Come in!"

The man who growled out these words, was a stoutly-built fellow of about five-and-thirty, in a black velveteen coat, very soiled drab breeches, lace-up half-boots, and grey cotton stockings, which enclosed a very bulky pair of legs.

"Come in, d'ye hear?" growled this engaging ruffian.

A white shaggy dog, with his face scratched and torn in twenty different places, skulked into the room.

"Why didn't you come in afore?" said the man. "You're getting too proud to own me afore company, are you? Lie down!" This command was accompanied with a kick, which sent the animal to the other end of the room. He appeared well used to it, however; for he coiled himself up in a corner very quietly and, winking his very ill-looking eyes about twenty times in a minute, appeared to occupy himself in taking a survey of the apartment. . . .

In the obscure parlour of a low public house, in the filthiest part of Little Saffron Hill there sat a man in a velveteen coat whom no experienced agent of police would have hesitated to recognise as Mr. William Sikes. At his feet, sat a white-coated, red-eyed dog; who occupied himself, alternately, in winking at his master with both eyes at the same time; and in licking a large, fresh cut on one side of his mouth.

"Keep quiet, you warmit! keep quiet!" said Mr. Sikes. Whether his meditations were so intense as to be disturbed by the dog's winking, or whether his feelings were so wrought upon by his reflections that they required all the relief derivable from kicking an unoffending animal to allay them, is a matter for argument. Whatever was the cause, the effect was a kick and a curse bestowed upon the dog simultaneously.

Dogs are not generally apt to revenge injuries inflicted upon them by their masters; but Mr. Sikes's dog, having faults of temper in common with his owner made no more ado but at once fixed his teeth in one of the half-boots. Having given it a hearty shake, he retired, growling, under a form; just escaping the pewter measure which Mr. Sikes levelled at his head. "You would, would you?" said Sikes, seizing the poker in one hand, and deliberately with the other a large clasp-knife. "Come here, you born devil! D'ye hear?"

The dog no doubt heard; but, appearing to entertain some unaccountable objection to having his throat cut, he remained where he was, and growled more fiercely than before: at the same time grasping the end of the poker and biting at it like a wild beast. This resistance only infuriated Mr. Sikes the more; who began to assail the animal most furiously; and the struggle was reaching a most critical point, when, the door suddenly opening, the dog darted out. . . .

"You are on the scent, are you, Nancy?" inquired Sikes.

"Yes, I am, Bill," replied the young lady; "and tired enough of it I am, too. The young brat's been ill and—"

Meanwhile, Oliver Twist was on his way to the bookstall; thinking how happy and contented he ought to feel; when he was startled by a young woman screaming out very loud, "Oh, my dear brother!" And he had hardly looked up, to see what the matter was, when he was stopped by having a pair of arms thrown tight round his neck. "What the devil's this?" said a man, bursting out of a beer-shop, with a white dog at his heels; "Young Oliver! Come home directly."

"I don't belong to them. Help! help!" cried Oliver, struggling in the man's powerful grasp. Rejoined the man, seizing Oliver by the collar, "Here, Bull's-eye, mind him, boy! Mind him!" Weak with recent illness; stupefied by the blows and the suddenness of the attack; terrified by the fierce growling of the dog, and the brutality of the man; what could one poor child do!

The narrow streets and courts, at length terminated in a large open space; scattered about which, were pens for beasts: and other indications of a cattle-market. They were in a dark corner. Oliver saw that resistance would be of no avail. He held out his hand which Nancy clasped tight in hers. "Give me the other," said Sikes. "Here, Bull's-eye!" The dog looked up, and growled. "See here, boy!" said Sikes, putting his other hand to Oliver's throat; "if he speaks ever so soft a word, hold him! D'ye mind!" The dog growled again; and, licking his lips, eyed Oliver as if he were anxious to attach himself to his windpipe without delay. Sikes, regarding the animal with a kind of grim and ferocious approval: "Now, you know what you've got to expect, master, so call away as quick as you like; the dog will soon stop that game." . . .

Oliver looked from one to the other [Sikes and Fagin], but when Bill Sikes concluded, he jumped suddenly to his feet, and tore wildly from the room, uttering shrieks for help. "Keep back the dog, Bill!" cried Nancy, springing before the door and closing it. "Keep back the dog; he'll tear the boy to pieces." "Serve him right!" cried Sikes, struggling to disengage himself from the girl's grasp. "Stand off from me, or I'll split your head against the wall." "I don't care for that, Bill," screamed the girl: "the child shan't be torn down by the dog, unless you kill me first." . . .

"Tell yer what?" asked the sleepy Noah.

"That about—NANCY," said the Jew, clutching Sikes by the wrist. "You followed her?"

"Yes." "To London Bridge?" "Yes." "Where she met two people?" "So she did." "A gentlemen, and a lady [Oliver's benefactors] that she had gone to of her own accord before, who asked her to give up all her pals, and to tell what house we meet at, which she did—did she not?" cried Fagin, half mad with fury. "All right," replied Noah.

"That's just what it was!" "Hell's fire!" cried Sikes, breaking fiercely from the Jew. "Let me go!" "You won't be—too—violent, Bill?" whined the Jew. "Be crafty, Bill, and not too bold."

Sikes dashed into the silent streets. Without one pause, but looking straight before him with savage resolution: he held on his course until he reached his own door; and entering his own room, double-locked the door, and drew back the curtain of the bed. The girl was lying, half-dressed, upon it. There was a candle burning, but the man hastily hurled it under the grate. "There's light enough for wot I've got to do." The robber sat regarding her, for a few seconds; and then, grasping her by the head and throat, dragged her into the middle of the room. "Bill, Bill for dear God's sake, for your own, for mine, stop before you spill my blood!" The housebreaker grasped his pistol, and he beat it twice with all the force he could summon upon the upturned face. She staggered and fell. The murderer seized a heavy club and struck her down. . . .

The sun burst upon the crowded city. If the sight had been a ghastly one in the dull morning, what was it, now, in all that brilliant light! Once he threw a rug over it; but it was worse to fancy the eyes moving towards him, than to see them glaring upward. And there was the body —mere flesh and blood, no more—but such flesh, and so much blood! The very feet of the dog were bloody. He moved, backward, towards the door: dragging the dog with him, lest he should soil his feet anew and carry out new evidences of the crime into the streets. It was a relief to have got free of the room. He whistled on the dog, and walked rapidly away. It was nine o'clock at night, when the man, quite tired out, and the dog, limping and lame from the unaccustomed exercise, turned down the hill by the church and crept into a small public-house. There was a fire in the tap-room, but he sat down in the furthest corner, and ate and drank with his dog: to whom he cast a morsel of food from time to time.

There was a shed that offered shelter for the night and here he stretched himself close to the wall. Now, a vision came before him, more terrible than that from which he had escaped. Those widely staring eyes, so lustreless and so glassy were everywhere. Suddenly there arose the noise of distant shouting. . . . He could hear the cry of Fire! There were people there. It was like new life to him. He darted onward—leaping gate and fence as madly as the dog, who careered with loud and sounding bark before him. Hither and thither he dived that night; never ceasing to engage himself wherever noise and men were thickest. Morning dawned. This mad excitement over, there returned, with tenfold force, the dreadful consciousness of his crime. The dog obeyed the significant beck of his finger, and they drew off, stealthily, together.

Suddenly, he took the desperate resolution of going back to London. The dog, though,—if any descriptions of him were out, it would not be forgotten that the dog was missing, and had probably gone with him. This might lead to his apprehension. He resolved to drown him, and walked on, looking about for a pond: picking up a heavy stone and tying it to his handkerchief as he went. The animal looked up into his master's face while these preparations were making; and, whether his instinct apprehended something of their purpose, or the robber's sidelong look at him was sterner than ordinary, he skulked a little farther in the rear than usual, and cowered as he came more slowly along. When his master halted at the brink of a pool, and looked round to call him, he stopped outright. "Come here!" cried Sikes. The animal came up from very force of habit; but as Sikes stooped to attach the handkerchief to his throat, he uttered a low growl and started back. "Come back!" said the robber. The dog wagged his tail, but moved not. Sikes made a running noose and called him again. The dog advanced, retreated, paused an instant, turned, and scoured away at his hardest speed. The man whistled again and again. But no dog appeared, and at length he resumed his journey. . . .

Beyond Dockhead, in the Borough of Southwark, stands Jacob's Island, surrounded by a muddy ditch. In Jacob's Island, the warehouses are roofless and empty; the walls are crumbling down; the doors are falling into the streets. The houses have no owners; they are entered upon by those who have the courage. In an upper room of one of these houses—ruinous in other respects, but strongly defended at door and window—there were assembled three men, who sat in gloomy silence: Toby Crackit, Mr. Chitling, and Kags.

Toby turned to Chitling and said, "When was Fagin took then?"

"Just at dinner-time—two o'clock this afternoon." The horror-stricken witness of this scene got up and paced violently to and fro. Whilst he was thus engaged, a pattering noise was heard upon the stairs, and Sikes's dog bounded into the room. They ran to the window, down stairs and into the street. The dog had jumped in at an open window; he made no attempt to follow them, nor was his master to be seen. "If he was coming here, he'd have come with the dog," said Kags, stooping down to examine the animal, who lay panting on the floor. "Here! Give us some water for him; he has run himself faint." "He's drunk it all up, every drop," said Chitling after watching the dog some time in silence. "Covered with mud—lame—half-blind—he must have come a long way." "Where can he have come from!" exclaimed Toby. "He" (none of them called the murderer by his old name) "He can't have made away with himself," said Chitling. "If he had," said Kags, "the dog 'ud want to lead us away to where he did it. No. I think he's got out of the country, and left the dog behind." This solution, appearing the most probable one, was adopted; and the dog, creeping under a chair, coiled himself up to sleep. They had sat thus, some time, when suddenly was heard a hurried knocking at the door below. Crackit went to the window, and, shaking all over, drew in his head. The dog too was on the alert in an instant, and ran whining to the door. Crackit went down to the door, and returned followed by a man; it was the very ghost of Sikes. "How came that dog here?" he asked. "Alone. Three hours ago." . . .

Then, came a loud knocking at the door, and then a hoarse murmur from such a multitude of angry voices as would have made the boldest quail. "Damn you!" cried the desperate ruffian, throwing up the sash and menacing the crowd. "Do your worst! I'll cheat you yet!"

"The tide," cried the murderer as he staggered back into the room, and shut the faces out, "the tide was in as I came up. Give me a rope, a long rope. They're all in front. I may drop into the Folly Ditch, and clear off that way. Give me a rope, or I shall do three more murders and kill myself at last." He looked over the low parapet. The water was out, and the ditch a bed of mud. The cries and shrieks of those who were pressed almost to suffocation, were dreadful; the narrow ways were completely blocked up; and the immediate attention was distracted from the murderer. Seeing this sudden change, he sprung upon his feet, determined to make one last effort for his life by dropping into the ditch, and, at the risk of being stifled, endeavouring to creep away in the darkness and confusion. Roused into new strength, he set his foot against the stack of chimneys, fastened one end of the rope firmly round it, and with the other made a strong running noose. He could let himself down by the cord to within a less distance of the ground than his own height, and had his knife ready to cut it then and drop.

At the very instant when he brought the loop over his head previous to slipping it beneath his arm-pits, the murderer, looking behind him on the roof, threw his arms above his head, and uttered a yell of terror. "The eyes again!" he cried. Staggering as if struck by lightning, he lost his balance and tumbled over the parapet. The noose was at his neck. It ran up with his weight, tight as a bow-string. He fell five-and-thirty feet. There was a sudden jerk, a terrific convulsion of the limbs; and there he hung. The murderer swung lifeless against the wall.

A dog, which had lain concealed till now, ran backwards and forwards on the parapet with a dismal howl, and, collecting himself for a spring, jumped for the dead man's shoulders. Missing his aim, he fell into the ditch, turning completely over as he went; and striking his head against a stone, dashed out his brains.

WALTER SAVAGE LANDOR'S *Pomero* AND *Giallo*

■ *During his long life as esteemed mid-nineteenth-century poet and man of letters, Landor had several dogs, including a shepherd in his early days. His favorite breed, however, was the Pomeranian, including Pomero, whose company he cherished for twelve years, and his last dog, Giallo. Like his impetuous Romantic contemporary Byron, Landor found dogs more trustworthy than men, and on being asked if dogs went to heaven, he replied, "Why not? They have all of the good and none of the bad qualities of man." The following extract on Pomero is by Landor's devoted friend and biographer, John Forster. The poem to Giallo is Landor's own.*

From A FRIEND NOT LITERARY, AND OTHER FRIENDS

Every autumn, as long as the last of Landor's sisters lived, took him [Landor] upon a visit to her in Warwick, at the house in which he was born; and the only drawback from his pleasure, on these as on all occasions when he quitted Bath, was his inability, through fear of accident or loss, to take with him a favorite companion, who may claim honorable mention in this history. "Daily," he wrote to me from Warwick in 1844, "do I think of Bath and Pomero. I fancy him lying on the narrow window-sill, and watching the good people go to church. He has not yet made up his mind between the Anglican and

Roman Catholic; but I hope he will continue in the faith of his forefathers, if it will make him happier." This was a small white Pomeranian dog that had been sent to him from his Fiesolan villa the previous autumn; visiting by the way myself, to whom he had been consigned for safer delivery; and at first sight fairly dazzling me, as I well remember, by the eager brightness of his eye and the feathery whiteness of his coat, as he pushed his nose through the wicker basket in which he had travelled the last stage of his journey. "Eighteen shillings for me, padrone," was the message sent me in Landor's next letter, informing me that already they were on speaking terms, and that I was to be reimbursed his fare from Florence. "He places his head between my knees to hear that part of the letter which concerns him personally. He barks terribly, and listens to no expostulation; but replies that he is a young creature, and ought to have his own way in consideration of it; finally, that his grandpapa kept up barking till the advanced age of seven." For many more years than seven the new friends were inseparable; and Landor's own figure, as it trudged up and down Bath streets, was not better known than his little bright-eyed companion's became. They were faces, both of them, that most people turned to look after; and Pomero certainly had the better coat. His master was quite conscious of this; and not long after his arrival told me, on sending me his "love and a bite," that the young rascal, not content with the advantage he already had, was always trying to make it greater. "He will have to pay at least half my tailor's bill, besides the mending of my new silk stockings. However, I do assure you he is well born. I have been making inquiries about it. There is not an older family in Bologna. His ancestors preceded the Bentivoglios, and were always stanch republicans."

"Pomero was on my knee," he says on another occasion to me, "when your letter came. He is now looking out of the window; a sad male gossip, as I often tell him. I dare not take him with me to London. He would most certainly be stolen, and I would rather lose Ipsley or Llanthony [estates of Landor's]. The people of the house love him like a child, and declare he is as sensible as a Christian. He not only is as sensible, but much more Christian than some of those who have lately brought strife and contention into the Church. Everybody knows him, high and low, and he makes me quite a celebrity." As time went on, his value to his master went far beyond Ipsley or Llanthony; for on asking whether he was inclined to part with him, "No, madam," was his answer, "not for a million of money!" "*Not for a million!*" she exclaimed; whereupon I added, "that a million would not make me at all happier, and that the loss of Pomero would make me miserable for life." Nor perhaps will the reader object to another mention of this little hero at the house of one of his master's earliest heroines and dearest friends, as I saw her myself in Bath, looking nearly as young as her grandchild. "Pomero is sitting in a state of contemplation, with his nose before the fire. He twinkles his ears and his feathery tail at your salutation. He now licks his lips and turns round, which means *Return mine.* The easterly wind has an evident effect on his nerves. Last evening I took him to hear Luisina de Sodre play and sing. She is my friend the Countess de Molande's granddaughter, and daughter of De Sodre, minister of Brazil to the Pope a few years ago. Pomero was deeply affected, and lay close to the pedal on her gown, singing in a great variety of tones, not always in time. It is unfortunate that he always *will* take a part where there is music, for he sings even worse than I do."

As his companion in morning calls, Landor took his faithful little friend more frequently; and one of the residents in Bath, a clever as well as kindly observer, has described one of his morning visits as an event to the friend he visited. I have myself been present at them, and can confirm the description. The favorite subject of conversation would be rather politics than literature; and during all the time of the visit the little animal would be lying under his chair, with front paws stretched out, sharp face flattened on them, and small ears restlessly moving to catch any remotest signal that this wearisome morning call was over. The glad intimation would come quite unexpectedly, when, on hearing suddenly from Landor, in the very middle of some frantic outburst of wrath or some heresy of wild extravagance, a word or two of caressing Italian, out from his chair would dart Pomero, rushing and leaping into his master's lap, and barking madly in the ecstasy of his joy. "I shall never survive thee, carissimo," Landor thereupon would say; to which, as the other barked a like glad promise, he would add, "I do not intend to live after him. If he dies, I shall take poison."

These touches will suffice, though hardly a letter now came from him that did not name the small fond creature: but I may add, that whenever his more intimate friends visited Bath in his absence, they were expected to see and report of Pomero "en pension"; and as the reception given to Kenyon on one of these occasions was pretty much that which all of us had, a few words from Landor shall describe it. "Kenyon tells me he saw Pomero at Bath, who turned his tail upon him; proud as a county candidate toward his constituents when he has just won his election. I shall reason with him on this, and tell him that *he* ought to know better, being somewhat more than country gentleman or a knight of a shire." The picture would hardly be complete without the contrast of how his master was received. "At six last night," wrote Landor to me the morning after one of his summer absences from Bath, "I arrived, and instantly visited Pomero *en pension*. His joy at seeing me amounted to madness. His bark was a scream of delight. He is now sitting on my head, superintending all I write, and telling me to give his love."

"Next to servants, horses are the greatest trouble in life. Dogs are blessings, true blessings. Pomero, who sends his love, is the comfort of my solitude and the delight of my life. He is quite a public character here in Bath. Everybody knows him and salutes him. He barks aloud at all—familiarly, not fiercely. He takes equal liberties with his fellow-creatures, if indeed dogs are more his fellow-creatures than I am. I think it was Saint Francis de Sales who called birds and quadrupeds his sisters and brothers. Few saints have been so good-tempered, and not many so wise." And in the same kindly spirit to all dumb creatures he speaks in another letter of field-sports. "Let men do these things if they will. Perhaps there is no harm in it; perhaps it makes them no crueler than they would be otherwise. But it is hard to take away what we cannot give; and life is a pleasant thing, at least to birds. No doubt the young ones say tender things one to another, and even the old ones do not dream of death."

The good, joyous, generous Kenyon died in December, 1856, thinking of his friends to the last. Yet why should I scruple to add another name? Landor had lost in this year also the little Pomeranian dog who had been for more than twelve years his constant and sprightly companion. "Pomero, dear Pomero died this evening" (10th March, 1856) "at about four o'clock. I have been able to think of nothing else." "Everybody in this house," he wrote a few days later, "grieves for Pomero. The cat lies day and night upon his grave; and I will not disturb the kind creature, though I want to plant some violets upon it, and to have his epitaph placed around his little urn.

> *O urna! nunquam sis tuo eruta hortule;*
> *Cor intus est fidele, nam cor est canis.*
> *Vale, hortule! aeternumque, Pomero! vale.*
> *Sed, si datur, nostri memor."*

[Of which a free translation might be:

> O urn! may you never be cast out of this little garden:
> The heart within you is faithful, for it is the heart of a dog.
> Farewell, little garden! and farewell forever, Pomero!
> Yet, if it is granted, we will be remembered.]

GIALLO

> Giallo! I shall not see thee dead,
> Nor raise a stone above thy head,
> For I shall go some years before,
> Where thou will leap at me no more.

ABRAHAM LINCOLN'S *Fice*

■ *Although Lincoln did not read widely, he explored avidly and discerningly the major English authors—especially Shakespeare. Returning after an absence of fifteen years to the part of Indiana where he had spent his childhood, Lincoln wrote Andrew Johnston, a literary correspondent who was a practicing lawyer in Quincy, Illinois, that "seeing it and its objects and inhabitants aroused feelings in me which were certainly poetry; though whether my expression of those feelings is poetry is quite another question." Lincoln sent him the only pieces of his poetry which are known to have been published and gave him permission to publish three cantos of "doggerel." However, only two cantos of "The Return," entitled "Reflections" and "The Maniac," were published anonymously in the Quincy Whig for May 5, 1847. It is quite probable that "The Bear Hunt" is the third canto, for Lincoln had told Johnston in the letter which contained the text for "The Maniac" that if he "should ever send another, the subject will be a 'Bear Hunt.'" In it he utilized the ballad meter of William Cowper's popular "Diverting History of John Gilpin" to describe a diverting American event of his own time. As in Faulkner's "The Bear," there is the ever-present small, snappish dog (fice or feist), to whom Lincoln typically finds a human counterpart.*

46

THE BEAR HUNT

A wild-bear chace, didst never see?
    Then hast thou lived in vain.
Thy richest bump of glorious glee,
    Lies desert in thy brain.

When first my father settled here,
    'Twas then the frontier line:
The panther's scream, filled night with fear
    And bears preyed on the swine.

But wo for Bruin's short lived fun,
    When rose the squealing cry;
Now man and horse, with dog and gun,
    For vengeance, at him fly.

A sound of danger strikes his ear;
    He gives the breeze a snuff:
Away he bounds, with little fear,
    And seeks the tangled *rough*.

On press his foes, and reach the ground,
    Where's left his half munched meal;
The dogs, in circles, scent around,
    And find his fresh made trail.

With instant cry, away they dash,
    And men as fast pursue;
O'er logs they leap, through water splash,
    And shout the brisk halloo.

Now to elude the eager pack,
    Bear shuns the open ground;
Through matted vines, he shapes his track
    And runs it, round and round.

The tall fleet cur, with deep-mouthed voice,
    Now speeds him, as the wind;

While half-grown pup, and short-legged fice,
    Are yelping far behind.

And fresh recruits are dropping in
    To join the merry *corps;*
With yelp and yell,—a mingled din—
    The woods are in a roar.

And round, and round the chace now goes,
    The world's alive with fun;
Nick Carter's horse, his rider throws,
    And more, Hill drops his gun.

Now sorely pressed, bear glances back,
    And lolls his tired tongue;
When as, to force him from his track,
    An ambush on him sprung.

Across the glade he sweeps for flight,
    And fully is in view.
The dogs, new-fired, by the sight,
    Their cry, and speed, renew.

The foremost ones, now reach his rear,
    He turns, they dash away;
And circling now, the wrathful bear,
    They have him full at bay.

At top of speed, the horse-men come,
    All screaming in a row.
"Whoop! Take him Tiger. Seize him Drum."
    Bang,—bang—the rifles go.

And furious now, the dogs he tears,
    And crushes in his ire.
Wheels right and left, and upward rears,
    With eyes of burning fire.

But leaden death is at his heart,
    Vain all the strength he plies.

And, spouting blood from every part,
    He reels, and sinks, and dies.

And now a dinsome clamor rose,
    'Bout who should have his skin;
Who first draws blood, each hunter knows,
    This prize must always win.

But who did this, and how to trace
    What's true from what's a lie,
Like lawyers, in a murder case
    They stoutly *argufy*.

Aforesaid fice, of blustering mood,
    Behind, and quite forgot,
Just now emerging from the wood,
    Arrives upon the spot.

With grinning teeth, and up-turned hair—
    Brim full of spunk and wrath,
He growls, and seizes on dead bear,
    And shakes for life and death.

And swells as if his skin would tear,
    And growls and shakes again;
And swears, as plain as dog can swear,
    That he has won the skin.

Conceited whelp! we laugh at thee—
    Nor mind, that not a few
Of pompous, two-legged dogs there be,
    Conceited quite as you.

ELIZABETH BARRETT BROWNING'S *Flush*

■ *The semi-invalid poet Elizabeth Barrett, isolated in her regimented London home in the mid-1840s by a domineering father, found solace in the devotion of the younger poet Robert Browning and in her spaniel, Flush, who was her inseparable companion for twelve years. Elizabeth's devotion to Flush and the quasi-rivalry of the dog and the suitor are reflected in the more than one hundred letters of Robert and Elizabeth's voluminous correspondence that mention Flush. They also chronicle his encounter with the dog banditti who were able to extract ransoms for the release of their captives, since dogs were not legal property in the 1840s and owners had no means of redress. Flush was in Elizabeth's arms when she met Robert in Hodgson's Bookshop for their furtive departure for Europe on September 28, 1846. Flush died in the summer of 1854 and was buried in a cellar beneath Casa Guidi, the home of the Brownings in Florence.*

FLUSH OR FAUNUS

You see this dog; it was but yesterday
I mused forgetful of his presence here
Till thought on thought drew downward tear on tear;
When from the pillow, where wet-cheeked I lay,
A head as hairy as Faunus, thrust its way
Right sudden against my face, two golden-clear

Great eyes astonished mine, a drooping ear
Did flap me on either cheek to dry the spray!
I started first, as some Arcadian,
Amazed by goatly god in twilight grove;
But, as the bearded vision closelier ran
My tears off, I knew Flush, and rose above
Surprise and sadness,—thanking the true Pan
Who, by low creatures, leads to heights of love.

Elizabeth Barrett to Robert Browning

MARCH 10, 1846

You would laugh to see me at my dinner . . Flush & me—Flush placing me in such an heroic confidence, that, . . after he had cast one discriminating glance on the plate, &, in the case of "chicken," wagged his tail with an emphasis, . . he goes off to the sofa, shuts his eyes & allows a full quarter of an hour to pass before he returns to take his share. Did you ever hear of a dog before who did not persecute one with beseeching eyes at mealtimes? And remember, this is not the effect of *discipline.* Also if another than myself happens to take coffee or break bread in the room here, he teazes straightway with eyes & paws, . . teazes like a common dog & is put out of the door before he can be quieted by scolding. But with *me* he is sublime! Moreover he has been a very useful dog in his time,—(in the point of capacity)— causing to disappear supererogatory dinners & impossible breakfasts which . . to do him justice, is a feat accomplished without an objection on his side, always.

APRIL 17, 1846

Today I went down stairs with Flush, he running before as when *we* walk together through the gate. I opened the drawingroom door; when instead of advancing he stopped short . . & I heard strange voices . . & then he drew back & looked up in my face exactly as if to say, "No! This will not do for us!—we had better go home again." Surely enough, visitors were in the room . . & he & I returned upon our steps. But think of his sense!—Flush beats us both in "common sense," dearest. Next to Flush we may be something, but Flush takes the *pas,* as when he runs down stairs.

This morning, Henrietta & I went as usual to Hodgson's and took possession of the chair in waiting, as Flush did of the whole territory, setting himself, with all the airs of a landed proprietor, to snap at the shop boy. Nota bene—Flush is likely to injure my popularity if I take him about with me much. He has been used, you see, to be "*Caesar* in his own house," & the transition of being Caesar everywhere is the easiest thing in the world. Yet as to leaving him at home, it is impossible, . . not to mention other objections!—His delight in going out in the carriage is scarcely a natural thing— Yesterday I was in the back drawingroom waiting to go out, and just said to him, "Flush! go & see if the carriage is come"—instantly he ran to the front windows, standing on his hind legs & looking up the street & down. Now Mr. Kenyon would declare that *that* was my invention. Yet it is the literal truth of history.

JUNE 2, 1846

Today I paid my first visit to Miss *Tripsack* . . a feast was spread for Arabel & Flush & me, which made me groan in the spirit, & Flush wag his tail, to look upon . . ice cream and cakes, which I was to taste & taste in despite of all memories of dinner an hour before. So I am glad I went—& so is Flush, who highly approves of that class of hospitable attentions, & wishes it were the way of the world every day.

JUNE 16, 1846

Lizzie & I & Flush took our places in the carriage & went to Hyde Park . . drove close by the Serpentine. Flush had his head out of the window the whole way . . except when he saw a long whip . . or had a frightful vision at the water of somebody washing a little dog . . which made him draw back into the carriage with dilated eyes & quivering ears, & set about licking my hands, for an 'Ora pro nobis.'

JUNE 18, 1846

Therefore I put on my bonnet, & called Flush, & walked down stairs & into the street all alone. And with just Flush, I walked there, up & down in a glorious independence. As to Flush, he frightened me a little & spoilt my vain-glory—for Flush has a very good, stout vain-glory of his own, &, although perfectly fond of me, has no idea whatever of being ruled over by me!—(he looks beautiful scorn out of his golden eyes, when I order him to do this or this) . . & *Flush* chose to walk on the opposite side of the street—he *would*,—he insisted on it! & every moment I expected him to disappear into some bag of the dog-stealers, as an end to *his* glory. Happily, however, I have no moral with which to point my tale—it's a very immoral story, & shows neither Flush nor myself punished for our sins.

JULY 9, 1846

Ah Flush, Flush!—he did not hurt you really? You will forgive him for me? The truth is that he hates all unpetticoated people & that though he does not hate *you,* he has a certain distrust of you, which any outward sign, such as the umbrella, reawakens—But if you had seen how sorry & ashamed he was yesterday!—I slapped his ears & told him that he never should be loved again: and he sate on the sofa (sitting, not lying) with his eyes fixed on me all the time I did the flowers, with an expression of quiet despair in his face. At last I said, 'If you are good, Flush, you may come & say that you are sorry' . . on which he dashed across the room &, trembling all over, kissed first one of my hands & then another, and put up his paws to be shaken, & looked into my face with such great beseeching eyes that you would certainly have forgiven him just as I did. It is not savageness. If he once loved you, you might pull his ears & his tail, & take a bone out of his mouth even, & he would not bite you. He has no savage caprices like other dogs & men I have known.

JULY 12, 1846

Flush had his foot pinched in shutting the cab-door, & though he cried piteously & held it up, looking straight to me for sympathy, no sooner had he touched the grass than he began to run without a thought of it. Flush always makes the most of his misfortunes—he is of the Byronic school—il se pose en victime.

JULY 22, 1846

As to Flush, he came up stairs with a good deal of shame in the bearing of his ears, & straight to me—no indeed! I would not speak to him. So he lay down on the floor at my feet looking from under his eyebrows at me—I did not forgive him till nearly eight oclock however.

ELIZABETH BARRETT BROWNING 53

And I have not yet given him your cakes. Almost I am inclined to think now that he has not *a soul*. To behave so to you!—Wicked Flush!—And *you*, so good and gentle to him! Anyone but *you*, would have said "hasty words" at least.

JULY 26, 1846

When Flush came into the room & had spoken to me (in the Flush-language) & had examined your chair, he suddenly fell into a rapture and reminded me that the cakes you left, were on the table. So I explained thoroughly to him that *you* had brought them for him, & that he ought to be properly ashamed therefore for his past wickedness, & make up his mind to love you & not bite you for the future—& then he was allowed to profit from your goodness to him. How *over-*good of you!

AUGUST 4, 1846

Flush thanks you! I asked him if he loved you even, & he wagged his tail. Generally when I ask him that question he won't answer at all, —but you have overcome him with generosity—as you do me!

AUGUST 23, 1846

When I opened my door on my return, Flush threw himself upon me with a most ecstatical agony, & for full ten minutes did not cease jumping & kissing my hands—he thought he had lost me for certain, this time. Oh! & you warn me against losing *him*. Indeed I take care —those "organized banditti" are a dreadful reality. Did I not tell you once that they had announced to me that I should not have Flush back the *next time*, for less than ten guineas—? But you will let him come with us to Italy, instead—will you not, dear, dearest? Because, if I leave him behind, he will be hanged for my sins in this house— or I could not be sure of the reverse of it—And even if he escaped that fate, consider how he would break his heart about me. Dogs pine to death sometimes—& if ever a dog loved a man, or a woman, Flush loves me.

SEPTEMBER 1, 1846

Here is a distress for me, dearest! I have lost my poor Flush—*lost* him. This morning Arabel & I, & he with us went in a cab to Vere Street & he followed us as usual into a shop and out of it again, & was at my heels when I stepped up into the carriage. Having turned, I said, 'Flush,' &—there was no Flush!—He had been caught up in that moment, from *under* the wheels & the thief must have run with him & thrown him into a bag perhaps. Henry went down for me directly to the Captain of the banditti, who evidently knew all about it. Henry told him that I was resolved not to give much—but of course they will make me give what they choose—My poor Flush!

SEPTEMBER 3, 1846

And then poor Flush! I have not got him back yet—no, indeed—The archfiend, Taylor, came last night to say that they would accept six pounds, six guineas, with half a guinea for himself & Papa desired Henry to refuse to pay, & not to tell me a word about it—all which I did not find out till this morning. Now it is less, as the money goes, than I had expected, and I was very vexed & angry, & wanted Henry to go at once & conclude the business—only he wouldn't, talked of Papa, & persuaded me that Taylor would come today with a lower charge—He has not come—and if people wont do as I choose, I shall go down tomorrow morning myself and bring Flush back with me—

SEPTEMBER 7, 1846

Only a few words to tell you that Flush is found, & lying on the sofa, with one paw & both ears hanging over the edge of it. Flush arrived here at eight oclock & the first thing he did was to dash up to this door, & then to drink his purple cup full of water, filled three times over. He was not so enthusiastic about seeing me, as I expected—he seemed bewildered & frightened—and whenever anyone said to him "Poor Flush, did the naughty men take you away?" he put up his head & moaned & yelled. Six guineas, was his ransom—& now I have paid twenty for him to the dog-stealers.

Elizabeth Barrett Browning to Miss Mitford

AUGUST 20, 1847

Flush hated Vallombrosa, and was frightened out of his wits by the pine forests. Flush likes civilised life, and the society of little dogs with turned-up tails, such as Florence abounds with. Unhappily it abounds also with *fleas*, which afflict poor Flush to the verge sometimes of despair. Fancy Robert and me down on our knees combing him with a basin of water on one side! He suffers to such a degree from fleas that I cannot bear to witness it. He tears off his pretty curls through the irritation. Do you know of a remedy?

FEBRUARY 22, 1848

My Flush is as well as ever, and perhaps gayer than ever I knew him. He runs out in the piazza whenever he pleases, and plays with the dogs when they are pretty enough, and wags his tail at the sentinels and civic guard, and takes the Grand Duke as a sort of neighbour of his, whom it is proper enough to patronise, but who has considerably less inherent merit and dignity than the spotted spaniel in the alley to the left.

APRIL 30, 1849

Flush's jealousy of the baby would amuse you. For a whole fortnight he fell into deep melancholy and was proof against all attentions lavished on him. Now he begins to be consoled a little and even condescends to patronise the cradle.

■ *Though Emily Brontë frequently alluded to her dog Keeper in her letters, she scarcely conveyed the closeness of the bond between them; and, like Emily Dickinson, she did not commemorate her dog in her poems. The most inclusive view of the relationship is provided by a contemporary author, Mrs. Elizabeth Gaskell, who visited the Brontë home at Haworth (in Yorkshire), and in her* Life of Charlotte Brontë *included comments on the other children of the ill-fated family.*

EMILY AND HER DOG "KEEPER"

Charlotte was more than commonly tender in her treatment of all dumb creatures, and they, with that fine instinct so often noticed, were invariably attracted towards her. The feeling, which in Charlotte partook of something of the nature of an affection, was, with Emily, more of a passion. Some one speaking of her to me . . . said, "she never showed regard to any human creature; all her love was reserved for animals." The helplessness of an animal was its passport to Charlotte's heart; the fierce, wild, intractability of its nature was what often recommended it to Emily. Speaking of her dead sister [Emily], the former told me that from her many traits in Shirley's character were taken; her way of sitting on the rug reading, with her arm round her rough bull-dog's neck; her calling to a strange dog, running past, with hanging head and lolling tongue, to give it a merciful draught of water, its

57

maddened snap at her, her nobly stern presence of mind, going right into the kitchen, and taking up one of Tabby's red-hot Italian irons to sear the bitten place, and telling no one, till the danger was well-nigh over, for fear of the terrors that might beset their weaker minds. All this, looked upon as a well-invented fiction in *Shirley*, was written down by Charlotte with streaming eyes; it was the literal true account of what Emily had done. The same tawny bull-dog (with his "strangled whistle"), called "Tartar" in *Shirley*, was "Keeper" in Haworth parsonage; a gift to Emily. With the gift came a warning. Keeper was faithful to the depths of his nature as long as he was with friends; but he who struck him with a stick or whip, roused the relentless nature of the brute, who flew at his throat forthwith, and held him there till one or the other was at the point of death. Now Keeper's household fault was this. He loved to steal up-stairs, and stretch his square, tawny limbs, on the comfortable beds, covered over with delicate white counterpanes. But the cleanliness of the parsonage arrangements was perfect; and this habit of Keeper's was so objectionable, that Emily, in reply to Tabby's remonstrances, declared that, if he was found again transgressing, she herself, in defiance of warning and his well-known ferocity of nature, would beat him so severely that he would never offend again. In the gathering dusk of an autumn evening, Tabby came, half triumphantly, half tremblingly, but in great wrath, to tell Emily that Keeper was lying on the best bed, in drowsy voluptuousness. Charlotte saw Emily's whitening face, and set mouth, but dared not speak to interfere; no one dared when Emily's eyes glowed in that manner out of the paleness of her face, and when her lips were so compressed into stone. She went up-stairs, and Tabby and Charlotte stood in the gloomy passage below, full of the dark shadows of coming night. Down-stairs came Emily, dragging after her the unwilling Keeper, his hind legs set in a heavy attitude of resistance, held by the "scuft of his neck," but growling low and savagely all the time. The watchers would fain have spoken, but durst not, for fear of taking off Emily's attention, and causing her to avert her head for a moment from the enraged brute. She let him go, planted in a dark corner at the bottom of the stairs; no time was there to fetch stick or rod, for fear of the strangling clutch at her throat—her bare clenched fist struck against his red fierce eyes, before he had time to make his spring, and in the language of the turf, she "punished him" till his eyes were swelled up, and the half-blind, stupefied beast was led to his accustomed lair, to have his swelled head fomented and cared for by the very

Emily herself. The generous dog owed her no grudge; he loved her dearly ever after; he walked first among the mourners to her funeral; he slept moaning for nights at the door of her empty room, and never, so to speak, rejoiced, dog fashion, after her death. He, in his turn, was mourned over by the surviving sister. Let us somehow hope, in half Red Indian creed, that he follows Emily now; and, when he rests, sleeps on some soft white bed of dreams, unpunished when he awakens to the life of the land of shadows.

EMILY DICKINSON'S *Carlo*

■ *Like her esteemed contemporary, poet Emily Brontë, Emily Dickinson did not celebrate her dog in verse. In her letters to various friends, however, she frequently alluded to Carlo; and though she gives little objective description of him, she provides enough details of his size and behavior to give him an identity as a real presence. In view of her isolated and restricted life, it is not surprising that she should have listed him as one of her three "companions"; for he was indeed an indispensable confidant to whom she could express herself freely, knowing he would not "tell."*

To Susan Gilbert Dickinson

26 SEPTEMBER 1858

Vinnie and I are pretty well. Carlo—comfortable—terrifying man and beast, with renewed activity—is cuffed some—hurled from piazza frequently, when Miss Lavinia's "flies" need her action elsewhere.

To Mrs. Samuel Bowles

10 DECEMBER 1859

I could make a balloon of a Dandelion, but the fields are gone. . . . If I built my house I should like to call you. I talk of all these things with Carlo, and his eyes grow meaning, and his shaggy feet keep a slower pace.

To "Master" (unknown recipient)

Could'nt Carlo, and you and I walk in the meadows an hour—and nobody care but the Bobolink—and *his*—a *silver* scruple?

To Colonel T. W. Higginson

25 APRIL 1862

You ask of my Companions. Hills—Sir—and the Sundown—and a Dog—large as myself, that my Father bought me—They are better than Beings—because they know—but do not tell. . . .

To Mrs. Samuel Bowles

SPRING 1862

Sue—draws her little Boy—pleasant days—in a Cab—and Carlo—walks behind, accompanied by a Cat. . . .

To Colonel T. W. Higginson

7 JUNE 1862

If fame belonged to me, I could not escape her—if she did not, the longest day would pass me on the chase—and the approbation of my Dog, would forsake me—then—My Barefoot-Rank is better—

To Colonel T. W. Higginson

AUGUST 1862

Of "shunning Men and Women"—they talk of Hallowed things, aloud—and embarrass my Dog—He and I don't object to them, if they'll exist their side. I think Carl[o] would please you—He is dumb, and brave—

To Samuel Bowles

AUGUST 1862

The Hills you used to love when you were in Northampton, miss their old lover, could they speak—and the puzzled look—deepens in Carlo's forehead, as Days go by, and you never come.

To Colonel T. W. Higginson

FEBRUARY 1863

I found you were gone [to war], by accident. . . . Carlo—still remained —and I told him—Best Gains—must have the Losses' Test—/ To constitute them—Gains—/ My Shaggy Ally assented—

To Louise and Frances Norcross

7 OCTOBER 1863

Dear Children, Nothing has happened but loneliness. . . . Carlo is consistent, has asked for nothing to eat or drink, since you went away. Mother thinks him a model dog, and conjectures what he might have been, had not Vinnie "demoralized" him.

To Colonel T. W. Higginson

EARLY JUNE, 1864

I was ill since September, and since April, in Boston, for a Physician's care— He does not let me go, yet I work in my Prison, and make Guests for myself—Carlo did not come, because that he would die, in Jail. . . .

To Colonel T. W. Higginson

LATE JANUARY, 1866

Carlo died—

To Colonel T. W. Higginson

EARLY 1866

Whom my Dog understood could not elude others.

Colonel T. W. Higginson

9 JUNE 1866

Thank you, I wish for Carlo.

DR. JOHN BROWN'S *Rab*

AND *Wasp*

■ *Dr. John Brown, a practicing physician in mid-nineteenth-century Edinburgh, was also an essayist who wrote one poignant story, "Rab and His Friends," about the powerful dog's long and quiet vigil at the hospital during the fatal illness of his mistress Ailie. The origins of the dog's devotion are described by Brown in his portrait of Rab. How particularly observant he was of canine behavior is also seen in his portrait of Wasp and her litter. Brown was active in attempts to diminish cruelty to animals and in providing shelters for stray dogs. Indeed, an editorial note to the first American edition (1861) of his work declared: "Dogs he loves with an enthusiasm to be found nowhere else in canine literature."*

RAB

Of Rab I have little to say, indeed have little right to speak of him as one of "our dogs"; but nobody will be sorry to hear anything of that noble fellow. Ailie, the day or two after the operation, when she was well and cheery, spoke about him, and said she would tell me fine stories when I came out, as I promised to do, to see her at Howgate. I asked her how James came to get him. She told me that one day she saw James coming down from Leadburn with the cart; he had been away west, getting eggs and butter, cheese and hens for Edinburgh. She saw he was in some trouble, and on looking, there was what she thought a young calf being dragged, or, as she called it, "haurled," at the back of the cart. James was in front, and when he came up, very warm and very angry, she saw that there was a huge young dog tied to the cart, struggling and pulling back with all his might, and as she said "lookin' fearsom." James, who was out of breath and temper, being past his time, explained to Ailie, that this "muckle brute o' a whalp" had been worrying sheep, and terrifying everybody up at Sir George Montgomery's at Macbie Hill, and that Sir George had ordered him to be hanged, which, however, was sooner said than done, as "the thief" showed his intentions of dying hard. James came up just as Sir George had sent for his gun and as the dog had more than once shown a liking for him, he said he "wad gie him a chance;" and so he tied him to his cart. Young Rab, fearing some mischief, had been entering a series of protests all the way, and nearly strangling himself to spite James and Jess, besides giving Jess more than usual to do. "I wish I had let Sir George pit that charge into him, the thrawn brute," said James. But Ailie had seen that in his foreleg there was a splinter of wood, which he had likely got when objecting to be hanged, and that he was miserably lame. So she got James to leave him with her, and go straight into Edinburgh. She gave him water, and by her woman's wit got his lame paw under a door, so that he couldn't suddenly get at her, then with a quick firm hand she plucked out the splinter, ...nd put in an ample meal. She went in some time after, taking no notice of him, and he came limping up, and laid his great jaws in her lap; from that moment they were "chief," as she said, James finding him mansuete and civil when he returned.

She said it was Rab's habit to make his appearance exactly half an hour before his master, trotting in full of importance, as if to say, "He's all right, he'll be here." One morning James came without him. He had left Edinburgh very early, and in coming near Auchindinny, at a lonely part of the road, a man sprang out on him, and demanded his money. James, who was a cool hand, said, "Weel a weel, let me get it," and stepping back, he said to Rab, "Speak till him, my man." In an instant Rab was standing over him, threatening strangulation if he stirred. James pushed on, leaving Rab in charge; he looked back, and saw that every attempt to rise was summarily put down. As he was telling Ailie the story, up came Rab with that great swing of his. It turned out that the robber was a Howgate lad, the worthless son of a neighbor, and Rab knowing him had let him cheaply off; the only thing, which was seen by a man from a field was, that before letting him rise, he quenched (*pro tempore*) the fire of the eyes of the ruffian, by a familiar Gulliverian application of Hydraulics, which I need not further particularize. James, who did not know the way to tell an untruth, or embellish anything, told me this as what he called "a fact *positeevely.*"

WASP

Was a dark brindled bull-terrier, as pure in blood as Cruiser or Wild Dayrell. She was brought by my brother from Otley, in the West Riding. She was very handsome, fierce, and gentle, with a small, compact, finely-shaped head, and a pair of wonderful eyes,—as full of fire and of softness as Grisi's; indeed she had to my eye a curious look of that wonderful genius—at once wild and fond. It was a fine sight to see her on the prowl across Bowden Moor, now cantering with her nose down, now gathered up on the top of a dyke, and with erect ears, looking across the wild like a moss-trooper out on business, keen and fell. She could do everything it became a dog to do, from killing an otter or a polecat, to watching and playing with a baby, and was as docile to her master as she was surly to all else. She was not quarrelsome, but "being in," she would have pleased Polonius as much, as in being "ware of entrance." She was never beaten, and she killed on the spot several of the country bullies who came out upon her when following her master in his rounds. She generally sent them off howling with one snap, but if this was not enough, she made an end of it.

But it was as a mother that she shone; and to see the gypsy, Hagarlike creature nursing her occasional Ishmael—playing with him, and fondling him all over, teaching his teeth to war, and with her eye and the curl of her lip daring any one but her master to touch him, was like seeing Grisi [probably the famous Italian soprano] watching her darling *"Gennaro,"* who so little knew why and how much she loved him.

Once when she had three pups, one of them died. For two days and nights she gave herself up to trying to bring it to life—licking it and turning it over and over, growling over it, and all but worrying it to awake it. She paid no attention to the living two, gave them no milk, flung them away with her teeth, and would have killed them, had they been allowed to remain with her. She was as one possessed, and neither ate, nor drank, nor slept, was heavy and miserable with her milk, and in such a state of excitement that no one could remove the dead pup.

Early on the third day she was seen to take the pup in her mouth, and start across the fields towards the Tweed, striding like a race-horse —she plunged in, holding up her burden, and at the middle of the stream dropped it and swam swiftly ashore; then she stood and watched the little dark lump floating away, bobbing up and down with the current, and losing it at last far down, she made her way home, sought out the living two, devoured them with her love, carried them one by one to her lair, and gave herself up wholly to nurse them; you can fancy her mental and bodily happiness and relief when they were pulling away—and theirs.

On one occasion my brother had lent her to a woman who lived in a lonely house, and whose husband was away for a time. She was a capital watch. One day an Italian with his organ came—first begging, then demanding money—showing that he knew she was alone and that he meant to help himself, if she didn't. She threatened to "lowse the dowg;" but as this was Greek to him, he pushed on. She had just time to set Wasp at him. It was very short work. She had him by the throat, pulled him and his organ down with a heavy crash, the organ giving a ludicrous sort of cry of musical pain. Wasp thinking this was from some creature within, possibly a *whittret*, left the ruffian, and set to work tooth and nail on the box. Its master slunk off, and with mingled fury and thankfulness watched her disembowelling his only means of an honest living. The woman good-naturedly took her off, and signed to the miscreant to make himself and his remains scarce. This he did with a scowl; and was found in the evening in the village, telling a series of lies to the watchmaker, and bribing him with a shilling to mend his pipes—"his kist o'whussels."

ELEANOR ATKINSON'S *Bobby*

■ *The countless thousands of readers of* Greyfriars Bobby *have no doubt been attracted not only by its touching theme of canine fidelity but also by its rich detail and the verisimilitude of its setting. Bobby lives in the 1860s and acts in a scene which is fully integrated with the narrarive, and the thousands of tourists that visit Edinburgh each year tend to include a view of Bobby's monument. Yet the book was not written by a native Scotswoman but by an American feature writer on the staff of the* Chicago Tribune. *Mrs. Atkinson wrote other similar novels, such as* Poilu, a Dog of Roubaix (1918).

From GREYFRIARS BOBBY

When the time-gun boomed from Edinburgh Castle, Bobby gave a startled yelp. He was a little country dog—the smallest and shaggiest of Skye terriers. That morning he had come to the weekly market with Auld Jock, a farm laborer. With the time-gun it was Auld Jock's custom to go up to a snug little restaurant patronized chiefly by the decent poor. There, in Ye Olde Greyfriars Dining-Rooms, owned by Mr. John Traill, and four doors beyond the kirkyard gate, was a cozy little inglenook that Auld Jock and Bobby had come to look upon as their own. At its back, a tiny-paned window looked into the ancient place of the dead. Bobby knew that the kirkyard was forbidden ground. Once, he had joyously chased a cat across the graves. The angry caretaker was instantly outside his little stone lodge by the gate and taking Auld Jock sharply to task. Master and dog were hustled outside the gate and into a rabble of jeering slum gamins.

During that first summer of his life Bobby and Auld Jock were inseparable. In some strange way, Bobby had been separated from Auld Jock that November morning. The tenant of Cauldbrae farm had driven the cart in himself. Immediately he had driven out again, leaving Auld Jock behind. Bobby might have been carried to the distant farm, but Auld Jock's absence discovered, Bobby dropped from the cart tail and faced right about. After an hour's hard run, Bobby found the Grassmarket. In the strangest place, Bobby came upon Auld Jock. In a broken-down carrier's cart, Auld Jock lay huddled in his greatcoat and breathing heavily. Bobby took a running leap to the top of the low boots, scrambled up into the cart, and barked once, sharply, in his ear. Auld Jock forgot that Bobby should not be there. Down came a shaking, hot old hand in a rough caress.

It was plain, even to Bobby, that something had gone wrong with Auld Jock. Given what was due him that morning and dismissed for the season, Auld Jock did not question the farmer's right to take Bobby "back hame." But Auld Jock parted with Bobby and with his courage, together.

A sweep of drenching rain brought the old man suddenly to his feet and by the urging of Bobby, Auld Jock came to Greyfriars Place. Mr. Traill stood bare-headed in his doorway. "Man, you're vera ill," he cried, sharply. "It's no' a doctor ye'll be needing, but physic an' a bed in the infirmary a day or twa." "I wullna gang to the infairmary an' tak' charity," said Auld Jock. "Whaur is it you have your lodging, Jock?" the landlord asked. He got the indefinite information that it was at the top of one of the tall, old tenements.

Auld Jock chuckled as he gained the last low level in this black hole of Edinburgh. Folk of every sort had preceded Auld Jock to his lodging nine gusty flights up. He had slept in this place for several winters. Lying together, man and dog fell into a sleep that was broken by Auld Jock's fitful coughing. It was not until the wind had long died to a muffled murmur, that Auld Jock slept soundly. He awoke late, stumbled dizzily to his feet and threw a sash back. "The snaw! Eh, Bobby, but it's a bonny sicht." He stooped to lift Bobby to the wonder of it, when the world suddenly went black and roaring around in his head. Staggering back he crumpled up in a pitiful heap on the floor.

Daylight had begun to fail when Auld Jock stirred, sat up, and taking from his pocket a leather purse, counted the few crowns and shillings. "There's eneugh," he said. All night Auld Jock was "aff 'is heid." After a long time he recognized the dog, patted the shaggy little head, and said between strangled breaths: "Puir—Bobby! Gang—awa' —hame—laddie."

Very early in the morning the flimsy door was quietly forced by authority. The motionless figure and peaceful face of the pious old shepherd had the dignity and beauty of some carven effigy in old Greyfriars kirkyard. "There's eneugh," a Burgh policeman said when the money was counted. He meant enough to save him from the last indignity—pauper burial. It was a Bible-reader who thought to look in the fly-leaf of Auld Jock's Bible. "His name is John Gray."

They laid him in a plain box of white deal. Bobby climbed on the top and stretched himself above his master. The humble funeral train went up to the kirkyard gate. The Bible-reader remained to see the grave partly filled in, and to try to persuade Bobby to go away with him. But the little dog resisted with such piteous struggles that the man put him down again. The caretaker in making his last rounds, picked Bobby up and set him over the wicket. Just before the closing hour a black-robed lady hurried through the wicket. Bobby slipped in behind her and after nightfall stretched himself prone across Auld Jock's grave.

After the report of the time-gun on Monday, Mr. Traill felt a tiny tug at his trouser-leg. The landlord stooped. "Gude dog to fetch Auld Jock—" With a faint cry, Bobby toppled over on the floor. It took Mr. Traill more than a moment to realize the nature of the trouble. Pale with pity, Mr. Traill snatched a plate of broth, set it under Bobby's nose, and watched him lap the warm liquid. As the short day darkened, Bobby trotted to the door.

Mr. Traill had no trouble at all keeping the little dog in sight to the kirkyard gate. Bobby plainly begged to have it opened. Bobby slipped through. Then, suddenly, as the door of the lodge opened and the caretaker came out, Bobby disappeared. "Whaur did the bit dog go?" demanded the landlord. "Weel, there was a bit tyke i' the kirkyaird twa days syne. I put 'im oot, an' haena seen 'im about ony mair. I mind, noo, it was some puir body frae the Coogate, wi' no' ony mourners but the sma' terrier aneath the coffin. Here's the place, Maister Traill; an' ye can see there's no' ony dog." "Ay, that would be Auld Jock and Bobby would no' be leaving him," insisted the landlord. He thought intently for a moment, and then spoke naturally, and much as Auld

Jock himself might have spoken. "Whaur are ye, Bobby? Come awa' oot, laddie!" Instantly the little dog stood before him. He had slipped from under the slab on which they were sitting. He came up to Mr. Traill confidingly, and looked pleadingly at the caretaker. Then he lay down on the mound. "I'll hae to put 'im oot." Mr. Traill went through the gateway calling back a challenge: "I daur you to do it."

At eight o'clock Mr. Trail found Bobby on the pavement. He followed the landlord up to the restaurant willingly and ate a light supper. Suddenly he trotted briskly off to a corner and crouched there. With a spring the rat was captured. In a position to ask fresh favors, the little dog was off to the door with cheerful staccato barks. His reasoning was as plain as print: "I hae done ye a service, noo tak' me back to the kirkyaird." Mr. Traill picked Bobby up. As he opened the door, he heard Geordie Ross's whistle. "Hey, laddie! he called. "Is there no' a way to smuggle the bit dog into the kirkyaird?" "Twa meenits' wark, sleekit footstaps, an' the fearsome deed is done," declared twelve-year-old Geordie.

Word had been left at all inns and markets for the tenant of Cauldbrae farm to call at Mr. Traill's place for Bobby. The man appeared on Wednesday. "There's a wee lassie wha wants Bobby for a pet. It wasna richt for Auld Jock to win 'im awa'." As Bobby stretched to an awakening, the farmer thrust him into a covered basket. When they reached Cauldbrae farm, an eager little voice cried out, "Hae ye got ma ain Bobby, faither?" A little gasp and a wee sob: "Is gude Auld Jock deid, daddy?"

Bobby refused to eat at first, but by and by ate a good supper in the lassie's company. Instantly Bobby was up, begging to be let out. "We'll juist hae to put 'im i' the byre wi' the coos for the nicht," cried the distracted mither. The single promise of escape was an inch-wide crack under the door. There he began to dig. Bobby's nose sniffed liberty. His back bruised and strained by the struggle, he stood, trembling with exhaustion, in the windy dawn. Bobby slipped out of the cow-yard. Suddenly, the wind brought a whiff of the acrid coal smoke of Edinburgh three miles away. As he neared the city the hour bells aided him. A night and a day of exhausting work, of anxiety and grief, had used up the last ounce of fuel. Bobby turned into Greyfriars Place and dashed to the kirkyard gate. When Bobby lay down on Auld Jock's grave, pellets of frozen snow were falling.

In Greyfriars kirkyard was work to be done that he could do. Now a big rat came out into the open. A leap and Bobby captured it. With the growing light grew the heap of the slain on Auld Jock's grave. When the lodge door was heard to open, he held his ground bravely. The caretaker was literally badgered and cajoled into following him. Bobby fixed his pleading eyes on the man while fate hung in the balance. "Gude wark! Losh! but ye're a deil o' a bit dog!" Except for two more forced returns and ingenious escapes from the sheep-farm, Bobby had lived in the kirkyard undisturbed for six months. The caretaker had neither the heart to put him out nor the courage to face the kirk officers with a plea for him to remain. When the time-gun boomed, Bobby was let out for his midday meal at Mr. Traill's and a run about the neighborhood. Bobby was host to the disinherited children of the tenements.

It was more than eight years after Auld Jock fled from the threat of a doctor that Mr. Traill's prediction, that his tongue would get him into trouble with the magistrates, was fulfilled. A Burgh policeman well known to Mr. Traill came in. By way of making conversation he remarked, "I didna ken ye had a dog, John." Mr. Traill answered with easy indulgence: "There's mony a thing you dinna ken, Davie." The good-humored sarcasm rankled in the policeman's breast. Very early the next morning he was standing before the door of Mr. Traill's place. "Here's a bit paper for ye." Through the legal verbiage Mr. Traill made out that he was summoned to appear in the Burgh court, to answer to the charge of owning, or harboring, one dog, upon which he had not paid the license tax of seven shillings. For all its absurdity it was no laughing matter. The civic bench was occupied by no less than the Lord Provost as chief. It was morning before Mr. Traill had a glimmer of an idea to take with him in this unlucky business. About the Burgh court there was little formality. Mr. Traill was asked if he meant to contradict the testimony of the officer. "Nae, your Honor. But the bit terrier is no' my ain dog. With due respect to your Honor, I must tak' an appeal to the Lord Provost. . . ."

Mr. Traill was thinking how he might best plead Bobby's cause with the Lord Provost. The note that was handed him [Mr. Traill] on leaving the Burgh Court the day before, had read: "Meet me in St. Giles at eight o'clock, and bring the wee Highlander with you."

Seven shullings! It was an enormous sum to the tenement bairn. While Ailie and Tammy were collecting the price of his ransom, Bobby was exploring the interior of old St. Giles. The Lord Provost watched him with an approving eye. "Gude morning, Mr. Traill. So that is the famous dog that has stood sentinel for more than eight years." The great man stooped and shook Bobby's lifted paw with grave courtesy. "I heard you from the doorway of the court-room, and sent up a note asking that the case be turned over to me for some exceptional disposal. Would you mind telling another man the tale? " . . .

Confused by the size of the old cathedral, these slum children went no farther. Suddenly they were all inside, Ailie clasping the dog and crying: "Bobby's no' deid! Oh, Maister Traill, Tammy's got the seven shullin's in 'is bonnet!" Such an astonishing pile of copper coins it was. The Lord Provost lifted Bobby to the pulpit, and spoke so all might understand. "Are ye kennin' what it is to gie the freedom o' the toon to grand folk?" He dived into this pocket and that, searching until he found a narrow band of new leather with holes and a buckle, and riveted fast in the middle was a shining brass plate. Tammy read the inscription aloud: GREYFRIARS BOBBY / FROM THE LORD PROVOST / 1867 LICENSED.

The music grew louder and came nearer. The first of the route-marching the Castle garrison practised on bright spring mornings was always a delightful surprise to small boys and dogs. A preoccupied lady opened the wicket and Bobby was off. Five miles out of the city the halt was called. Bobby trotted on up the slope. The farm-house of Cauldbrae lay on the level terrace, steeped in memories. Bobby made a tour of the sheepfold, the cow-yard, and byre where Auld Jock had played with him. By and by he came upon the lassie. In the next instant he knew her. Wary of her remembered endearments, Bobby kept a safe distance. In a moment he frisked and barked at Elsie's heels. But when the bugle sounded from below, he started for the door. Before he knew what happened he was inside the poultry-house. There was no time to be lost, for the drums began to beat the march. Bobby noisily dashed around the dark place, and there arose such wild squawkings as to bring the gude-wife out in alarm. She flung the door wide. Bobby shot through.

Bobby did not know when the bridge-approach was passed; and then, on Castle Hill, he was in an unknown region. Bobby was off, up the curving roadway into the Castle. The officer of the day recognized the attractive little Skye and asked about him. Sergeant Scott explained that Bobby was living in Greyfriars kirkyard. If the little dog took a fancy to garrison life, he thought Mr. Traill, who had the best claim upon him, might consent to his transfer to the Castle. After orders, he would take Bobby down to the restaurant himself.

The sun had dropped behind the western Highlands. Bobby thought it quite time to go home. A red-coated guard paced on the other side of a closed gate. At every turn his efforts to escape from the Castle had been baffled. Avoiding lighted buildings and voices, he sped from shadow to shadow and explored the walls of solid masonry. Twenty minutes before, the May Light could be seen far out on the edge of the ocean. But now, the lights below had vanished. The highest ones expired in the rising fog. The Island Rock appeared to be sinking in a waveless sea of milk. The sergeant and the guest were out in time to see Bobby go over the precipice. Without any sound at all, Bobby dropped out of sight.

Foot by foot he went down, with no guidance at all; his feet were torn and pierced by splinters of rock and thorns. He leaped and fell stunned. When he tried to get up his hind legs refused to serve him. He rolled down the last slope of Castle Rock. Bobby had literally to drag himself now. Had not the gate to the kirkyard been left on the latch, he would have had to lie there until morning. But the gate gave way. He dragged himself through it and stretched himself on Auld Jock's grave.

In the misty dawn he lay very still, even when a pair of arms tried to lift his dead weight. When he tried to stand up he cried out with the pains and sank down again. After his lacerated feet had been cleaned and tied up, Bobby was a very comfortable wee dog, who enjoyed his breakfast of broth and porridge.

At the end of five years the leal Highlander was not only still remembered, but had become a local celebrity. It seemed, therefore, the most natural thing when the greatest lady in England, beside the Queen, the Baroness Burdett-Coutts, came all the way from London to see Bobby. Bobby captured her heart at once and led her to Auld Jock's grave. When she was seated on the table-tomb, he stood under her caress. In a week she returned to the churchyard; the Lord Provost was with her. She meant to ask to be allowed to do an unheard-of thing. "I want to put up a monument to the nameless man who inspired so much love, and to the little dog that was capable of giving it." Permission was given for a suitable memorial opposite the main gateway to the kirkyard.

What form the memorial was to take was not decided upon until two chance happenings one morning. The Grand Leddy had come down to watch the artist at work. Bobby was found sitting on the table-tomb, looking up toward the Castle.

His attitude might have meant anything or nothing, for the man who looked at him from above could not see his expression. All at once he realized that to see Bobby a human being must get down to his level. Then he set the wee Highlander up on an altar-topped shaft. Bobby continued to gaze up wistfully upon this masterless world. The image of the simple memorial was clear in her mind. As she was getting into her carriage a noble collie, with a hanging tongue, came out of Forest Road. He had done a hard morning's work and had hunted far and unsuccessfully for water. The lady turned into Greyfriars Dining Rooms, and asked Mr. Traill for a basin of water. After a thoughtful moment Lady Burdett-Coutts said: "The suitable memorial here, Mr. Traill, is a fountain, with a low basin level with the curb, and a higher one, and Bobby sitting on an altar-topped column above, looking through the kirkyard gate. It shall be his mission to bring men and small animals together in sympathy by offering both water." Then the carriage rolled away.

The caretaker's voice was husky. "Ye're an auld dog, Bobby. Ye'll juist hae to sleep i' the hoose the misty nicht." Bobby went up to the lodge with the old couple. But when the door was held open for him, he wagged his tail in farewell. All the concession he was willing to make to old age and bad weather was to sleep under the fallen table tomb.

FRED GIPSON'S *Old Yeller*

■ *This novel is one of Gipson's many regional narratives based on legends of the hill country of frontier Texas in the 1860s. These legends were passed on to Gipson by his mother and father, to whom he dedicates the book. The distinctive character of the picaresque and courageous dog and his depiction through the language and perspective of a fourteen-year-old boy give the novel a worthy place in the tradition of* Huckleberry Finn. *Disney's cinematic treatment of* Old Yeller *has further endeared him to mid-twentieth-century youngsters and many adults.*

From OLD YELLER

We called him Old Yeller. The name had a sort of double meaning. One part meant that his short hair was a dingy yellow, a color that we called "yeller" in those days. The other meant that when he opened his head, the sound he let out came closer to being a yell than a bark. I [Travis] remember like yesterday how he strayed in out of nowhere to our log cabin on Birdsong Creek. He made me so mad at first I wanted to kill him.

The minute I opened the door and looked up, I saw that the meat was gone. I looked down then. At that same instant, a dog rose from where he'd been curled up on the ground. He was a big ugly yeller dog. One short ear had been chewed clear off and his tail had been bobbed so close to his rump that there was hardly stump enough to wag. But the most noticeable thing to me about him was how thin and starved looking he was, all but for his belly. His belly was swelled up as tight and round as a pumpkin. It wasn't hard to tell how come that belly was so full. Well, to lose the only meat we had left from last winter's hog butchering was bad enough. But what made me even madder was the way the dog acted. He rose to his feet, stretched, yawned, then came romping toward me, wiggling that stub tail and yelling *Yow! Yow! Yow!* Just like he belonged there and I was his best friend. "Why, you thieving rascal!" I shouted and kicked at him as hard as I could. He ducked, just in time, so that I missed him by a hair. But nobody could have told I missed, after the way he fell over on the ground and lay there, with his belly up and his four feet in the air, squawling and bellering at the top of his voice. From the racket he made, you'd have thought I had a club and was breaking every bone in his body.

Then out came Little Arliss. He was hollering "A dog! A dog! You quit kicking my dog! You kick my dog, and I'll wear you to a frazzle!" . . .

I rode toward the cabin feeling proud of myself as a hunter and provider for the family. Let Arliss keep the thieving rascal. I guessed I could provide enough meat for him, too. Then suddenly, I felt different. That's when I found Little Arliss in the pool again. And in there with him was the big yeller dog. That dirty stinking rascal, romping around in our drinking water! I didn't give him a chance to get to me. I was too quick about jumping off the mule and grabbing up some rocks. I was lucky. The first rock I threw caught the big dog right between the eyes. And just as he came to his feet again, I caught him in the ribs with another one. He turned tail then and took out for the house, squawling and bawling. But I wasn't the only good rock thrower in the family. Arliss was only five years old, but I had spent a lot of time showing him how to throw a rock. Now I wished I hadn't. Because about then, a rock nearly tore my left ear off. Well, when you're fourteen years old, you can't afford to mix in a rock fight with your five-year-old brother. All I could do was turn tail like the yeller dog and head for the house, yelling for Mama.

I hung the fresh cuts of venison up in the dog run, right where Old Yeller had stolen the hog meat the night he came. I figured if he stole more of our meat, Mama would have to see that he was too sorry and no account to keep. But Old Yeller was too smart for that. He gnawed around on some of the deer's leg bones that Mama threw away; but not once did he ever even act like he could smell the meat we'd hung up. . . .

The bulls crashed into the cabin again. Mama came running to grab me by the arm. "Call the dog!" she said. Well, that was a real good idea. Here was a chance for that old yeller dog to pay back for all the trouble he'd made around the place. I ducked out and around the corner calling, "Here, Yeller! Here Yeller! Get 'em, boy! Sic 'em!" But he didn't come and he didn't sic 'em. He took one look at me running toward him with that bullwhip in my hand and knew I'd come to kill him. He tucked his tail and lit out in a yelling run for the woods. If there had been any way I could have done it, right then is when I would have killed him. . . .

Little Arliss made a practice of trying to catch and keep every living thing that ran, flew, jumped, or crawled. Then, after the yeller dog came, Little Arliss started catching even bigger game. Like cottontail rabbits and chaparral birds and a baby possum. Of course, it was Old Yeller that was doing the catching. He'd run the game down and turn it over to Little Arliss. Then Little Arliss could come in and tell Mama a big fib about how he caught it himself. . . .

Little Arliss's second scream was louder and shriller than the first. I raced out into the open. There was Little Arliss, down in that spring hole holding on to the hind leg of a little black bear cub, too scared to let go. Now what mattered was the bear cub's mama. She was coming so fast that she had the brush popping and breaking as she crashed through and over it. And no matter how fast Mama ran or how fast I ran, the bear was going to get there first! Then, just as the bear went lunging up the creek bank toward Little Arliss and her cub, a flash of yellow came streaking out of the brush. It was that big yeller dog. He was roaring like a mad bull. He wasn't one-third as big and heavy as the she bear, but when he piled into her from one side, he rolled her clear off her feet. They went down in a wild roaring tangle of twisting bodies and scrambling feet and slashing fangs. As I raced past them, I saw the bear lunge up to stand on her hind feet while she clawed at the body of the yeller dog hanging to her throat. I didn't wait to see more. I ran in and jerked Little Arliss loose from the cub. I grabbed him and slung him toward Mama like he was a half-empty sack of corn. I screamed at Mama. "Grab him, Mama. Grab him and run!" Then I heard Mama calling: "Come away from there, Travis. Hurry, son! Run!"

That spooked me. Up till then, I'd been ready to tie into that bear myself. Now, suddenly, I was scared out of my wits again. I ran toward the cabin. But like it was, Old Yeller nearly beat me there. Mama said that the minute that Old Yeller saw we were all in the clear and out of danger, he threw the fight to the bear and lit out for the house. But if the big yeller dog was scared or hurt, he sure didn't show it like we all did. All he did was come bounding in to jump on us and lick us in the face and bark so loud the noise nearly made us deaf. The way he acted, you might have thought that bear fight hadn't been anything more than a rowdy romp we'd all taken part in for the fun of it. After that, I couldn't do enough for Old Yeller. He'd pitched in and saved Little Arliss when I couldn't possibly have done it, and that was enough for me. . . .

Bud Searcy was a red-faced man who liked to visit around the settlement [and who had] a little white-haired granddaughter. Her name was Lisbeth and she came with her grandpa the day he visited us. He told how some strange varmit had recently started robbing the settlement blind. Or maybe it was even some*body*. Nobody could tell for sure. All they knew was that they were losing meat out of their smokehouses, eggs out of their hens' nests, and sometimes even whole pans of cornbread set out to cool. Listening to this, I got an uneasy feeling. Lisbeth motioned me to follow her off down to the spring. "It's him."

"What do you mean?" I said.

"I mean it's your big yeller dog," she said. "I saw him."

"Do what?" I asked.

"Steal that bait of ribs," she said. "I saw him get a bunch of eggs, too. But I'm not going to tell," she said.

"Why?"

"Because Miss Prissy is going to have pups. That's the name of my dog and your dog will be their papa, and I wouldn't want their papa to get shot." After Bud Searcy finally rode off home with Lisbeth riding behind him, I went and gathered the eggs and held three back. I called Old Yeller from the house and broke the eggs on a flat rock and tried to get him to eat them. He acted like he never heard tell that eggs were fit to eat. "You thievin' rascal," I said. . . .

The man's name was Burn Sanderson. He said he couldn't afford to hire riders, and so he'd brought along a couple of dogs to help him herd his cattle. One of these dogs, the best one, had disappeared.

"A big yeller dog?" Mama asked, looking sober and worried.

"Yessum," the man said, then added with a grin, "and the worst egg sucker and camp robber you ever laid eyes on. Steal you blind, that old devil will, but there was never a better cow dog born."

Mama turned to me. "Son, call Old Yeller," she said. I stood frozen in my tracks.

"Travis!"

Mama's voice was too sharp. I knew I was whipped.

"Now, Mrs. Coates," he said to Mama, "I can make out without him until your man comes."

But Mama shook her head. The man tied his rope around Old Yeller's neck and mounted his horse. That's when Little Arliss caught onto what was happening. He grabbed up a bunch of rocks and went to throwing them. One hit Sanderson's horse in the flank. The horse went to pitching and bawling and grunting. This excited Old Yeller. He chased after the horse, baying him at the top of his voice.

When Sanderson finished riding the pitch out of his scared horse, he hollered at Old Yeller. Then he rode back toward us, wearing a wide grin. He swung down from his saddle. He came and got Little Arliss and loved him up till he hushed screaming. Then he said: "Look, boy, do you really want that thieving old dog?" Finally, Little Arliss nodded. "All right," Sanderson said, "but you've got to do something for me. Now, if you could talk your mama into feeding me a real jam-up meal of woman-cooked grub, I think it would be worth at least a one-eared yeller dog. Don't you?"

After dinner, he said his thank-yous to Mama and told me to come with him. At the spring, he slipped the bits out of his horse's mouth, then turned to me. "Now boy," he said, "I didn't want to tell your mama. But there's a plague of hydrophobia making the rounds, and I want you to be on the lookout for it."

The next day, I went to rounding up and marking hogs and forgot all about the plague. Old Yeller's yelling bay told me that he'd caught up with the hogs. They'd found a place where the flood waters had undercut one of the dirt banks to form a shallow cave. No amount of barking and pestering by Old Yeller could get them out. I went back and stood on the bank above them. It wouldn't be easy to reach beneath that undercut bank and rope a pig, but I believed it could be done. I took my rope from around my waist and moved to the lip of the cutbank. I reached back under and picked up the first pig. I drew him up. A second pig moved out from the back part of the cave. I made my cast, and that's when it happened. The dirt bank broke beneath my weight. A wagon load of sand caved off and spilled down over the angry hogs. I went with the sand. I could never get to my feet in time to escape the rush of angry hogs roaring down upon me.

It was Old Yeller who saved me. He flung himself between me and the killer hogs. He yelled with pain as the savage tushes ripped into him. He took the awful punishment meant for me. He gave me that one-in-a-hundred chance to get free. I took it. In wild terror, I ran till a forked stick tripped me and I fell.

Then I got hold of myself again. When I set out, I just kept walking till I found him. He lay in the dry wash. He'd tried to follow me, but was too hurt to keep going. He was holed up under a broad slab of red sandstone. I'd have missed him if he hadn't whined as I walked past. He grunted and groaned as he dragged himself toward me. He sank back to the ground, his blood-smeared body trembling while he wiggled his stub tail and tried to lick my hog-cut leg. Here he was, trying to lick my wound, when he was bleeding from a dozen worse ones. And worst of all was his belly. It was ripped wide open and some of his insides were bulging out through the slit. Carefully, I eased his entrails back into place. Then I pulled the lips of the wound together and wound strips of my shirt around Yeller's body. I slid Old Yeller back under the rock slab. I reached in and let him lick my hand. "Yeller," I said, "I'll be back. I'm promising that I'll be back." Then I lit out for home in a limping run. . . .

For the next couple of weeks, Old Yeller and I had a rough time of it. I lay on the bed inside the cabin and Yeller lay on the cowhide in the dog run, and we both hurt so bad that we were wallowing and groaning and whimpering all the time. I heard a quiet step at the door. It was Lisbeth. "I brung you a surprise. One of Miss Prissy's pups!" But right now all I wanted was just to quit hurting.

I heard Mama calling to Spot as she went out to the cowpen. A little later, I heard Spot beller like a fighting bull. Mama slammed the door shut. "Spot made fight at me," she said. "It was like I was some varmit that she'd never seen before." In the next few days, while Old Yeller and I healed fast, we all worried and watched. When the bull came, he reeled and staggered like he couldn't see where he was going. Right then, for the first time since we'd brought him home, Old Yeller came up off his cowhide bed. He rose, with a savage growl. He moved out toward the bull, so trembly weak that he could hardly stand. Now, I knew that Spot wouldn't get well, and this bull wouldn't either. I knew they were both deathly sick with hydrophobia. Old Yeller had scented that sickness in this bull and somehow sensed how fearfully dangerous it was. I thought of Lisbeth and Little Arliss down past the spring. "Mama!" I said, "Bring me my gun. That bull! He's mad with hydrophobia and he's heading straight for Lisbeth and Little Arliss."

By this time, Old Yeller was there, baying the bull, keeping out of his reach, but ready to eat him alive. I didn't wait to see more. I hobbled down and shot the roan bull between the eyes.

As soon as the job of burning the bull was over, Mama told us we had to do the same for the Spot heifer. I waited till she came stumbling across the sandy bed of the wash, then fired, dropping her in the middle of it. By the time I got back, I was dead beat. Mama told me to get to bed. "We'll go start the burning," she said. So I told Mama where to find Spot and watched her and Lisbeth head out, both mounted on Jumper. Yeller went trotting after them. It wasn't until dark came that I really began to get uneasy. I'd just about made up my mind to go look for Mama and Lisbeth when I heard the sound of dogs fighting. Also, I recognized the voice of Old Yeller. It was the sort of raging yell he let out when he was in a fight to the finish. Then I heard Jumper snorting keenly and Mama calling in a frightened voice, "Travis! Travis! Make a light, Son, and get your gun. And hurry!" I ran and snatched up four bunches of bear-grass and dumped the bunches in a pile outside the yard fence, then hurried to bring a live coal from the fireplace to start them burning. A little flame started, then leaped high with a roar. I caught my first glimpse of the screaming, howling battle. It was Old Yeller, all right, tangled with some animal as big and savage as he was. Mama called from outside the light's rim. "Careful, Son. And take close aim; it's a big loafer wolf, gone mad." I held fire while I hollered at Mama, "Y'all get in the cabin."

Old Yeller and the big wolf fought there in the firelight. Then they went down in a tumbling roll that stopped with the big wolf on top, his huge jaws shut tight on Yeller's throat. I squeezed the trigger. For a second, I just knew that I'd killed Old Yeller, too. Then, he heaved a big sort of sigh and struggled up to start licking my hands and wagging that stub tail. I was so relieved that I slumped to the ground and was sitting there, shivering, when Mama came and sat down beside me. "He had to've been mad, son," Mama wound up. "You know that no wolf in his right senses would have acted that way." "Yessum," I said, "and it's sure a good thing that Old Yeller was along to keep him fought off."

Mama waited a little bit, then said in a quiet voice: "It was a good thing for us, son; but it wasn't good for Old Yeller."

"What do you mean?" I said. "Old Yeller's all right. He's maybe chewed up some, but he can't be bad hurt."

Then it hit me what Mama was getting at. All my insides froze.

"But Mama!" I cried out. "Old Yeller's just saved your life! He's saved my life. He's saved Little Arliss's life! We can't—" Mama got up and put her arms across my shoulder again. "I know son," she said. "But he's been bitten by a mad wolf."

"But Mama," I said, "We don't know for certain."

"We can't take a chance, Son," she sobbed. "It would be you or me or Little Arliss or Lisbeth next. I'll shoot him if you can't."

It came clear to me that Mama was right. It was going to kill something inside me to do it. Once I knew for sure I had it to do I was just numb all over, like a dead man walking. Quickly, I left Mama and went to stand in the light of the burning bear grass. I reloaded my gun and called Old Yeller back from the house. I stuck the muzzle of the gun against his head and pulled the trigger.

Days went by, and I couldn't seem to get over it. I couldn't eat, I couldn't sleep, I couldn't cry. Hurting worse than I'd ever hurt in my life. Mama tried to talk to me about it, and I let her. Lisbeth talked to me. She pointed out that I had another dog, the speckled pup. "He's part Old Yeller," she said.

Then one night it rained till daylight. That seemed to wash away the hydrophobia plague, [and] the next morning Papa came riding home [from Kansas] through the mud [with] a saddle horse for me. I didn't feel one way or another about the horse. That went on for a week or better before a thing happened that brought me alive again. I heard a shrieking yelp, and out of the kitchen door came the speckled pup with a big chunk of cornbread clutched in his mouth. Right then, I began to feel better. Tomorrow, I thought, I'll take Arliss and that pup out for a squirrel hunt. If he was big enough to act like Old Yeller, he was big enough to start learning to earn his keep.

JOHN MUIR'S *Stickeen*

■ *When the renowned naturalist John Muir toured the eastern states near the end of the past century, he reported on his recent explorations of Alaskan glaciers. As a kind of anecdotal variation, one must suppose, he included the part played by his lone companion, a small mongrel dog whose name, Stickeen, derived from an Alaskan river and Indian tribe. Much against Muir's will, Stickeen had insisted on following him. To many in Muir's audiences the little dog soon loomed larger than glacial topography, and wherever Muir went he was asked to retell the story of Stickeen's stubborn fidelity. As a result Muir's friend Richard Watson Gilder, editor of* The Century *magazine, persuaded Muir to permit its publication therein. (It was republished in 1909 in a small volume entitled* Stickeen.*) The episode, indeed, has not only its dramatic moments in which death is risked but also its mutual revelations between man and dog which left their mark on both of them. The insistent courage which motivated an unfamiliar mongrel to endure bitter weather and the crossing of awesome crevasses so puzzled Muir that he constantly pondered the dog's inscrutable behavior. His observations constitute one of the most informative insights into and tributes to the canine character in American literature. Transcending his early image as a nuisance, Stickeen had become (to use Muir's final word) "immortal."*

From AN ADVENTURE WITH A DOG
AND A GLACIER

In the summer of 1880 I set out from Fort Wrangel in a canoe with
the Rev. S. H. Young, my former companion, and a crew of Indians,
to continue the exploration of the icy region of south-eastern Alaska,
begun in the fall of 1870. Mr. Young, for whom we were waiting, at
length came aboard, followed by a little black dog that immediately
made himself at home by curling up in a hollow among the baggage.
I like dogs, but this one seemed so small, dull, and worthless that I
objected to his going, and asked the missionary why he was taking
him. "Such a helpless wisp of hair will only be in the way," I said;
"you had better pass him up to one of the Indian boys on the wharf,
to be taken home to play with the children. This trip is not likely to
be a good one for toy dogs. He will be rained on and snowed on for
weeks, and will require care like a baby." But the missionary assured
me that he was a perfect wonder of a dog—could endure cold and
hunger like a polar bear, could swim like a seal, and was wondrous
wise, etc., making out a list of virtues likely to make him the most
interesting of the company.

Nobody could hope to unravel the lines of his ancestry. He was
short-legged, bunchy-bodied, and almost featureless—something like
a muskrat. Though smooth, his hair was long and silky, so that when
the wind was at his back it ruffled, making him look shaggy. At first
sight his only noticeable feature was his showy tail, which was about
as shady and airy as a squirrel's and was carried curling forward nearly
to his ears. On closer inspection you might see his thin, sensitive ears
and his keen dark eyes with cunning tan spots. Mr. Young told me that
when the dog was about the size of a wood-rat he was presented to his
wife by an Irish prospector at Sitka, and that when he arrived at Fort
Wrangel he was adopted by the Stickeen Indians as a sort of new
good-luck totem, and named "Stickeen" for the tribe, with whom he
became a favorite. On our trip he soon proved himself a queer character: odd, concealed, independent, keeping invincibly quiet, and doing
many inexplicable things that piqued my curiosity. Sailing week after
week through the long, intricate channels and inlets among the innumerable islands and mountains of the coast, he spent the dull days in
sluggish ease, motionless, and apparently as unobserving as a hibernat-
ing marmot. But I discovered that somehow he always knew what was
going forward. When the Indians were about to shoot at ducks or seals,

or when anything interesting was to be seen along the shore, he would rest his chin on the edge of the canoe and calmly look out. When he heard us talking about making a landing, he roused himself to see what sort of place we were coming to, and made ready to jump overboard and swim ashore as soon as the canoe neared the beach. Then, with a vigorous shake to get rid of the brine in his hair, he went into the woods to hunt small game. But though always the first to get out of the canoe, he was always the last to get into it. When we were ready to start he could never be found, and refused to come to our call. We soon found out, however, that though we could not see him at such times, he saw us, and from the cover of the briers and huckleberry-bushes in the fringe of the woods was watching the canoe with wary eye. For as soon as we were fairly off, he came trotting down the beach, plunged into the surf, and swam after us, knowing well that we would cease rowing and take him in. When the contrary little vagabond came alongside, he was lifted by the neck, held at arm's length a moment to drip, and dropped aboard. We tried to cure him of this trick by compelling him to swim farther before stopping for him; but this did no good: the longer the swim, the better he seemed to like it.

Though capable of most spacious idleness, he was always ready for excursions or adventures of any sort. When the Indians went into the woods for a deer, Stickeen was sure to be at their heels, provided I had not yet left camp. For though I never carried a gun, he always followed me, forsaking the hunting Indians, and even his master, to share my wanderings. The days that were too stormy for sailing I spent in the woods, or on the mountains or glaciers; and Stickeen always insisted on following me, gliding though the dripping huckleberry-bushes and prickly *Panax* and *Rubus* tangles like a fox, scarce stirring their close-set branches, wading and wallowing through snow, swimming ice-cold streams, jumping logs and rocks and the crusty hummocks and crevasses of glaciers with the patience and endurance of a determined mountaineer, never tiring or getting discouraged. Once he followed me over a glacier the surface of which was so rough that it cut his feet until every step was marked with blood; but he trotted on with Indian fortitude until I noticed his pain and, taking pity on him, made him a set of moccasins out of a handkerchief. But he never asked help or made any complaint, as if, like a philosopher, he had learned that without hard work and suffering there could be no pleasure worth having.

Yet nobody knew what Stickeen was good for. He seemed to meet danger and hardships without reason, insisted on having his own way, never obeyed an order, and the hunters could never set him on anything against his will, or make him fetch anything that was shot. I tried hard to make his acquaintance, guessing there must be something in him; but he was as cold as a glacier, and about as invulnerable to fun, though his master assured me that he played at home, and in some measure conformed to the usages of civilization. His equanimity was so immovable it seemed due to unfeeling ignorance. Let the weather blow and roar, he was as tranquil as a stone; and no matter what advances you made, scarce a glance or a tail-wag would you get for your pains. No superannuated mastiff or bulldog grown old in office surpassed this soft midget in stoic dignity. He sometimes reminded me of those plump, squat, unshakable cacti of the Arizona deserts that give no sign of feeling. A true child of the wilderness, holding the even tenor of his hidden life with the silence and serenity of nature, he never displayed a trace of the elfish vivacity and fun of the terriers and collies that we all know, nor of their touching affection and devotion. Like children, most small dogs beg to be loved and allowed to love, but Stickeen seemed a very Diogenes, asking only to be let alone. He seemed neither old nor young. His strength lay in his eyes. They looked as old as the hills, and as young and as wild. I never tired looking into them. It was like looking into a landscape; but they were small and rather deep-set, and had no explaining puckers around them to give out particulars. I was accustomed to look into the faces of plants and animals, and I watched the little sphinx more and more keenly as an interesting study. But there is no estimating the wit and wisdom concealed and latent in our lower fellow-mortals until made manifest by profound experiences; for it is by suffering that dogs as well as saints are developed and made perfect.

At length we discovered the entrance of what is now called Taylor Bay, and about five o'clock reached the head of it, and encamped near the front of a large glacier which extends as an abrupt barrier all the way across from wall to wall of the inlet, a distance of three or four miles. On first observation the glacier presented some unusual features, and that night I planned a grand excursion for the morrow. I awoke early, called not only by the glacier, but also by a storm. Rain, mixed with trailing films of scud and the ragged, drawn-out nether surfaces of gray clouds, filled the inlet, and was sweeping forward in a thick, passionate, horizontal flood, as if it were all passing over the country instead of falling on it. Everything was streaming with life and motion —woods, rocks, waters, and the sky. The main perennial streams were booming, and hundreds of new ones, born of the rain, were descending in gray and white cascades on each side of the inlet, fairly streaking their rocky slopes, and roaring like the sea. I had intended making a cup of coffee before starting, but when I heard the storm I made haste to join it. So I took my ice-ax, buttoned my coat, put a piece of bread in my pocket, and set out. Mr. Young and the Indians were asleep, and so, I hoped, was Stickeen; but I had not gone a dozen rods before he left his warm bed in the tent, and came boring through the blast after me. That a man should welcome storms for their exhilarating music and motion, and go forth to see God making landscapes, is reasonable enough; but what fascination could there be in dismal weather for this poor, feeble wisp of a dog, so pathetically small? Anyhow, on he came, breakfastless, through the choking blast. I stopped, turned my back to the wind, and gave him a good, dissuasive talk. "Now don't," I said, shouting to make myself heard in the storm—"now don't, Stickeen. What has got into your queer noddle now? You must be daft. This wild day has nothing for you. Go back to camp and keep warm. There is no game abroad—nothing but weather. Not a foot or wing is stir-ring. Wait and get a good breakfast with your master, and be sensible for once. I can't feed you or carry you, and this storm will kill you." But nature, it seems, was at the bottom of the affair; and she gains her ends with dogs as well as with men, making us do as she likes, driving us on her ways, however rough. So after ordering him back again and again to ease my conscience, I saw that he was not to be shaken off; as well might the earth try to shake off the moon. I had once led his master into trouble, when he fell on one of the topmost jags of a mountain, and dislocated his arms. Now the turn of his humble com-panion was coming. The dog just stood there in the wind, drenched and blinking, saying doggedly, "Where thou goest I will go." So I told him to come on, if he must, and gave him a piece of the bread I had put in my pocket for breakfast. Then we pushed on in company, and thus began the most memorable of all my wild days. The level flood, driving straight in our faces, thrashed and washed us wildly until we got into the shelter of the trees and ice-cliffs on the east side of the glacier, where we rested and listened and looked on in comfort.

When the wind began to abate I traced the east side of the glacier. All the trees standing on the edge of the woods were barked and bruised, showing high ice-mark in a very telling way, while tens of thousands of those that had stood for centuries on the bank of the glacier farther out lay crushed and being crushed. In many places I could see, down fifty feet or so beneath, the margin of the glacier mill, where trunks from one to two feet in diameter were being ground to pulp against outstanding rock-ribs and bosses of the bank. About three miles above the front of the glacier, I climbed to the surface of it by means of ax-steps, made easy for Stickeen; and as far as the eye could reach, the level, or nearly level, glacier stretched away indefinitely beneath the gray sky, a seemingly boundless prairie of ice. For a mile or two out I found the ice remarkably safe. The marginal crevasses were mostly narrow, while the few wider ones were easily avoided by passing around them, and the clouds began to open here and there. Thus encouraged, I at last pushed out for the other side; for nature can make us do anything she likes, luring us along appointed ways for the fulfilment of her plans. Toward the west side we came to a closely crevassed section, in which we had to make long, narrow tacks and doublings, tracing the edges of tremendous longitudinal crevasses, many of which were from twenty to thirty feet wide, and perhaps a thousand feet deep, beautiful and awful. In working a way through them I was severely cautious, but Stickeen came on as unhesitatingly as the flying clouds. Any crevasse that I could jump he would leap without so much as halting to examine it. The weather was bright and dark, with quick flashes of summer and winter close together. But Stickeen seemed to care for none of these things, bright or dark, nor for the beautiful wells filled to the brim with water so pure that it was nearly invisible, the rumbling, grinding moulins, or the quick-flashing, glinting, swirling streams in frictionless channels of living ice. Nothing seemed novel to him. He showed neither caution nor curiosity. His courage was so unwavering that it seemed due to dullness of perception, as if he were only blindly bold; and I warned him that he might slip or fall short. His bunchy body seemed all one skipping muscle, and his peg legs appeared to be jointed only at the top.

We gained the west shore in about three hours, the width of the glacier here being about seven miles. When we were about two miles from the west shore the clouds dropped misty fringes, and snow soon began to fly. Then I began to feel anxiety as to finding a way in the storm through the intricate network of crevasses which we had entered. Stickeen showed no fear. He was still the same silent, sufficient, uncomplaining Indian philosopher. When the storm-darkness fell he kept close behind me. The snow warned us to make haste, but at the same time hid our way. At rare intervals the clouds thinned and mountains, looming in the gloom, frowned and quickly vanished. I pushed on as best I could, jumping innumerable crevasses, and for every hundred rods or so of direct advance traveling a mile in doubling up and down in the turmoil of chasms and dislocated masses of ice. After an hour or two of the work we came to a series of longitudinal crevasses of appalling width, like immense furrows. These I traced with firm nerve, excited and strengthened by the danger, making wide jumps, poising cautiously on the dizzy edges after cutting hollows for my feet, before making the spring, to avoid slipping or any uncertainty on the farther sides, where only one trial is granted—exercise at once frightful and inspiring. Stickeen flirted across every gap I jumped, seemingly without effort. Many a mile we thus traveled, mostly up and down, making but little real headway in crossing, most of the time running instead of walking, as the danger of spending the night on the glacier became threatening. No doubt we could have weathered the storm for one night, and I faced the chance of being compelled to do so; but we were hungry and wet, and the north wind was thick with snow and bitterly cold, and of course that night would have seemed a long one. Stickeen gave me no concern. He was still the wonderful, inscrutable philosopher, ready for anything. I could not see far enough to judge in which direction the best route lay, and had simply to grope my way in the snow-choked air and ice. Again and again I was put to my mettle, but Stickeen followed easily, his nerves growing more unflinching as the dangers thickened; so it always is with mountaineers.

At length our way was barred by a very wide and straight crevasse, which I traced rapidly northward a mile or so without finding a crossing or hope of one, then southward down the glacier about as far, to where it united with another crevasse. In all this distance of perhaps two miles there was only one place where I could possibly jump it; but the width of this jump was nearly the utmost I dared attempt, while the danger of slipping on the farther side was so great that I was loath to try it. Furthermore, the side I was on was about a foot higher than the other, and even with this advantage it seemed dangerously wide. One is liable to underestimate the width of crevasses where the magnitudes in general are great. I therefore measured this one again and again, until satisfied that I could jump it if necessary, but that in case I should be compelled to jump back to the higher side, I might fail. I compelled myself to sit down and deliberate. Retracing my devious path in imagination, as if it were drawn on a chart, I saw that I was recrossing the glacier a mile or two farther up-stream, and was entangled in a section I had not before seen. Should I risk this dangerous jump, or try to regain the woods on the west shore, make a fire, and have only hunger to endure while waiting for a new day? At length, because of the dangers already behind me, I determined to venture against those that might be ahead, jumped, and landed well, but with so little to spare that I more than ever dreaded being compelled to take that jump back from the lower side. Stickeen followed, making nothing of it. But within a distance of a few hundred yards we were stopped again by the widest crevasse yet encountered. Of course I made haste to explore it, hoping all might yet be well. About three fourths of a mile up-stream it united with the one we had just crossed, as I feared it would. Then, tracing it down, I found it joined the other great crevasse at the lower end, maintaining a width of forty to fifty feet. We were on an island about two miles long and from one hundred to three hundred yards wide, with two barely possible ways of escape—one by the way we came, the other by an almost inaccessible sliver-bridge that crossed the larger crevasse from near the middle of the island. After tracing the brink, I ran back to the sliver-bridge and cautiously studied it. This one was evidently very old, for it had been wasted until it was the worst bridge I ever saw. The width of the crevasse was here about fifty feet, and the sliver, crossing diagonally, was about seventy feet long, was depressed twenty-five or thirty feet in the middle, and the up-curving ends were attached to the sides eight or ten feet below the surface of the glacier. Getting down the nearly vertical wall to the end of it and up the other side were the main difficulties, and they seemed all but insurmountable. Of the many perils encountered in my years of wandering in mountain altitudes, none seemed so plain and stern and merciless as this. And it was presented when we were wet to the skin and hungry, the sky was dark with snow, and the night near, and we had to fear the snow in our eyes and the disturbing action of the wind in any movement we might make. But we were forced to face it. It was a tremendous necessity.

Beginning not immediately above the sunken end of the bridge, but a little to one side, I cut nice hollows on the brink for my knees to rest in; then, leaning over, with my short-handled ax cut a step sixteen or eighteen inches below, which, on account of the sheerness of the wall, was shallow. That step, however, was well made; its floor sloped slightly inward, and formed a good hold for my heels. Then, slipping cautiously upon it, and crouching as low as possible, with my left side twisted toward the wall, I steadied myself with my left hand in a slight notch, while with the right I cut other steps and notches in succession, guarding against glinting of the ax, for life or death was in every stroke, and in the niceness of finish of every foothold. After the end of the bridge was reached, it was a delicate thing to poise on a little platform which I had chipped on its up-curving end, and, bending over the slippery surface, get astride of it. Crossing was easy, cutting off the sharp edge with careful strokes, and hitching forward a few inches at a time, keeping my balance with my knees pressed against its sides. The tremendous abyss on each side I studiously ignored. The surface of that blue sliver was then all the world. But the most trying part of the adventure was, after working my way across inch by inch, to rise from the safe position astride that slippery strip of ice, and to cut a ladder in the face of the wall—chipping, climbing, holding on with feet and fingers in mere notches. At such times one's whole body is eye, and common skill and fortitude are replaced by power beyond our call of knowledge. Never before had I been so long under deadly strain. How I got up the cliff at the end of the bridge I never could tell. The thing seemed to have been done by somebody else. I never have had contempt of death, though in the course of my explorations I often-times felt that to meet one's fate on a mountain, in a grand cañon, or in the heart of a crystal glacier would be blessed as compared with death from disease, a mean accident in a street, or from a sniff of sewer gas. But the sweetest, cleanest death, set thus calmly and glaringly clear before us, is hard enough to face, even though we feel gratefully sure that we have already had happiness enough for a dozen lives.

But poor Stickeen, the wee, silky, sleekit beastie—think of him! When I had decided to try the bridge, and while I was on my knees cutting away the rounded brow, he came behind me, pushed his head past my shoulder, looked down and across, scanned the sliver and its approaches with his queer eyes, then looked me in the face with a startled air of surprise and concern, and began to mutter and whine, saying as plainly as if speaking with words, "Surely you are not going to try that awful place?" This was the first time I had seen him gaze deliberately into a crevasse or into my face with a speaking look. That he should have recognized and appreciated the danger at the first glance showed wonderful sagacity. Never before had the quick, daring midget seemed to know that ice was slippery, or that there was such a thing as danger anywhere. His looks and the tones of his voice when he began to complain and speak his fears were so human that I uncon-sciously talked to him as I would to a boy, and in trying to calm his fears perhaps in some measure moderated my own. "Hush your fears, my boy," I said, "we will get across safe, though it is not going to be easy. No right way is easy in this rough world. We must risk our lives to save them. At the worst we can only slip; and then how grand a grave we shall have! And by and by our nice bones will do good in the terminal moraine." But my sermon was far from reassuring him; he began to cry, and after taking another piercing look at the tremendous gulf, ran away in desperate excitement seeking some other crossing. By the time he got back, baffled, of course, I had made a step or two. I dared not look back, but he made himself heard; and when he saw that I was certainly crossing, he cried aloud in despair. The danger was enough to daunt anybody, but it seems wonderful that he should have been able to weigh and appreciate it so justly. No mountaineer could have seen it more quickly or judged it more wisely, discriminating between real and apparent peril.

After I had gained the other side he howled louder than ever, and after running back and forth in vain search for a way of escape, he would return to the brink of the crevasse above the bridge, moaning and groaning as if in the bitterness of death. Could this be the silent, philosophic Stickeen? I shouted encouragement, telling him the bridge was not so bad as it looked, that I had left it flat for his feet, and he could walk it easily. But he was afraid to try it. Strange that so small an animal should be capable of such big, wise fears! I called again and again in a reassuring tone to come on and fear nothing; that he could come if he would only try. Then he would hush for a moment, look again at the bridge, and shout his unshakable conviction that he could never, never come that way; then lie back in despair, as if howling: "Oh-o-o, what a place! No-o-o; I can never go-o-o down there!" His natural composure and courage had vanished utterly in a tumultuous storm of fear. Had the danger been less, his distress would have seemed ridiculous. But in this gulf—a huge, yawning sepulcher big enough to hold everybody in the territory—lay the shadow of death, and his heartrending cries might well have called Heaven to his help. Perhaps they did. So hidden before, he was transparent now, and one could see the workings of his mind like the movements of a clock out of its case. His voice and gestures were perfectly human, and his hopes and fears unmistakable, while he seemed to understand every word of mine. I was troubled at the thought of leaving him. It seemed impossible to get him to venture. To compel him to try by fear of being left, I started off as if leaving him to his fate, and disappeared back of a hummock; but this did no good, for he only lay down and cried. So after hiding a few minutes, I went back to the brink of the crevasse, and in a severe tone of voice shouted across to him that now I must certainly leave him —I could wait no longer, and that if he would not come, all I could promise was that I would return to seek him next day. I warned him that if he went back to the woods the wolves would kill him, and finished by urging him once more by words and gestures to come on. He knew very well what I meant, and at last, with the courage of despair, hushed and breathless, he lay down on the brink in the hollow I had made for my knees, pressed his body against the ice to get the advantage of the friction, gazed into the first step, put his little feet together, and slid them slowly down into it, bunching all four in it, and almost standing on his head. Then, without lifting them, as well as I could see through the snow, he slowly worked them over the edge of the step, and down into the next and the next in succession in the same way, and gained the bridge. Then lifting his feet with the regularity and slowness of the vibrations of a seconds' pendulum, as if counting and measuring one, two, three, holding himself in dainty poise, and giving separate attention to each little step, he gained the foot of the cliff, at the top of which I was kneeling to give him a lift should he get within reach. Here he halted in dead silence, and it was here I feared he might fail, for dogs are poor climbers. I had no cord. If I had had one, I would have dropped a noose over his head and hauled him up. But while I was thinking whether an available cord might be made out of clothing, he was looking keenly into the series of notched steps and finger-holds of the ice-ladder I had made, as if counting them and fixing the position of each one in his mind. Then suddenly up he came, with a nervy, springy rush, hooking his paws into the notches and steps so quickly that I could not see how it was done, and whizzed past my head, safe at last!

And now came a scene! "Well done, well done, little boy! Brave boy!" I cried, trying to catch and caress him; but he would not be caught. Never before or since have I seen anything like so passionate a revulsion from the depths of despair to uncontrollable, exultant, triumphant joy. He flashed and darted hither and thither as if fairly demented, screaming and shouting, swirling round and round in giddy loops and circles like a leaf in a whirlwind, lying down and rolling over and over, sidewise and heels over head, pouring forth a tumultuous flood of hysterical cries and sobs and gasping mutterings. And when I ran up to him to shake him, fearing he might die of joy, he flashed off two or three hundred yards, his feet in a mist of motion; then, turning suddenly, he came back in wild rushes, and launched himself at my face, almost knocking me down, all the time screeching and screaming and shouting as if saying, "Saved! saved! saved!" Then away again, dropping suddenly at times with his feet in the air, trembling, and fairly sobbing. Such passionate emotion was enough to kill him. Who could have guessed the capacity of the dull, enduring little fellow for all that most stirs this mortal frame? Nobody could have helped crying with him.

But there is nothing like work for toning down either excessive fear or joy. So I ran ahead, calling him, in as gruff a voice as I could command, to come on and stop his nonsense, for we had far to go, and it would soon be dark. Neither of us feared another trial like this. Heaven would surely count one enough for a lifetime. The ice ahead was gashed by thousands of crevasses, but they were common ones. The joy of deliverance burned in us like fire, and we ran without fatigue, every muscle, with immense rebound, glorying in its strength. Stickeen flew across everything in his way, and not till dark did he settle into his normal foxlike, gliding trot. At last the mountains crowned with spruce came in sight, looming faintly in the gloaming, and we soon felt the solid rock beneath our feet, and were safe. Then came weariness. We stumbled down along the lateral moraine in the dark, over rocks and tree-trunks, through the bushes and devil-club thickets and mossy logs and boulders of the woods where we had sheltered ourselves in the morning. Then out on the level mud-slope of the terminal moraine. Danger had vanished, and so had our strength. We reached camp about ten o'clock, and found a big fire and a big supper. A party of Hoona Indians had visited Mr. Young, bringing a gift of porpoise-meat and wild strawberries, and hunter Joe had brought in a wild goat. But we lay down, too tired to eat much, and soon fell into a troubled sleep. The man who said, "The harder the toil the sweeter the rest," never was profoundly tired. Stickeen kept springing up and muttering in his sleep, no doubt dreaming that he was still on the brink of the crevasse; and so did I—that night and many others, long afterward, when I was nervous and overtired.

Thereafter Stickeen was a changed dog. During the rest of the trip, instead of holding aloof, he would come to me at night when all was quiet about the camp-fire, and rest his head on my knee, with a look of devotion, as if I were his god. And often, as he caught my eye, he seemed to be trying to say, "Wasn't that an awful time we had together on the glacier?"

MATTHEW ARNOLD'S *Kaiser*

■ *In his final fifteen years Arnold had enough leisure and space to enjoy (and spoil) his several dogs. Although his earlier elegy to the dachshund Geist ("At Geist's Grave") is the most often reprinted of his poems involving dogs, it does not project the dog's distinctive character as convincingly as "Kaiser Dead," written the year before Arnold's death. The mongrel Kaiser was clearly an exuberant companion and a somewhat unpredictable hedonist who brightened the last years of Arnold's life.*

KAISER DEAD
April 6, 1887

> WHAT, Kaiser dead? The heavy news
> Post-haste to Cobham calls the Muse,
> From where in Farringford she brews
>   The ode sublime,
> Or with Pen-bryn's bold bard pursues
>   A rival rhyme.
>
> Kai's bracelet tail, Kai's busy feet,
> Were known to all the village-street.
> "What, poor Kai dead?" say all I meet;
>   "A loss indeed!"
> O for the croon pathetic, sweet,
>   Of Robin's reed!

Six years ago I brought him down,
A baby dog, from London town;
Round his small throat of black and brown
    A ribbon blue,
And vouch'd by glorious renown
    A dachshound true.

His mother, most majestic dame,
Of blood-unmix'd, from Potsdam came;
And Kaiser's race we deem'd the same—
    No lineage higher.
And so he bore the imperial name.
    But ah, his sire!

Soon, soon the days conviction bring.
The collie hair, the collie swing,
The tail's indomitable ring,
    The eye's unrest—
The case was clear; a mongrel thing
    Kai stood confest.

But all those virtues, which commend
The humbler sort who serve and tend,
Were thine in store, thou faithful friend.
    What sense, what cheer!
To us, declining tow'rds our end,
    A mate how dear!

For Max, thy brother-dog, began
To flag, and feel his narrowing span.
And cold, besides, his blue blood ran,
    Since, 'gainst the classes,
He heard, of late, the Grand Old Man
    Incite the masses.

Yes, Max and we grew slow and sad;
But Kai, a tireless shepherd-lad,
Teeming with plans, alert, and glad
    In work or play,
Like sunshine went and came, and bade
    Live out the day!

Still, still I see the figure smart—
Trophy in mouth, agog to start,
Then, home return'd, once more depart;
    Or prest together
Against thy mistress, loving heart,
    In winter weather.

I see the tail, like bracelet twirl'd,
In moments of disgrace uncurl'd,
Then at a pardoning word re-furl'd,
    A conquering sign;
Crying, "Come on, and range the world,
    And never pine."

Thine eye was bright, thy coat it shone;
Thou hadst thine errands, off and on;
In joy thy last morn flew; anon,
    A fit! All's over;
And thou art gone where Geist hath gone,
    And Toss, and Rover.

Poor Max, with downcast, reverent head,
Regards his brother's form outspread;
Full well Max knows the friend is dead
    Whose cordial talk,
And jokes in doggish language said,
    Beguiled his walk.

And Glory, stretch'd at Burwood gate,
Thy passing by doth vainly wait;
And jealous Jock, thy only hate,
    The chiel from Skye,
Lets from his shaggy Highland pate
    Thy memory die.

Well, fetch his graven collar fine,
And rub the steel, and make it shine,
And leave it round thy neck to twine,
    Kai, in thy grave.
There of thy master keep that sign,
    And this plain stave.

WILLIAM FAULKNER'S *Lion*

■ *William Faulkner's fictional Yoknapatawpha County of the 1880s is conspicuously filled by animals—mules, spotted horses, bears, dogs, and livestock. In part through their presence life becomes a contest continuously in touch with the elemental but also humanized and redeemed by a Faulknerian code of pride, honor, courage, and compassion. In "The Bear," as Faulkner remarks, "only Sam [Fathers], Old Ben, and the mongrel Lion were taintless and incorruptible." Man, bear, and dog singlemindedly fulfill their diverse natures.*

From THE BEAR

There was a man and a dog too this time. Two beasts, counting Old Ben, the bear, and two men, counting Boon Hoggenbeck, in whom some of the same blood ran which ran in Sam Fathers, and only Sam and Old Ben and the mongrel Lion were taintless and incorruptible.

He [Isaac McCaslin] was sixteen. For six years now he had been a man's hunter. It had begun on that day when his cousin McCaslin brought him for the first time to the camp. He had already inherited then, without ever having seen it, the big old bear that had earned for himself a name, like a living man:—the long legend of corn-cribs broken down and rifled, of shoats and pigs and even calves carried bodily into the woods and devoured and dogs mangled and slain. For the first time he realised that the bear which had run in his listening and loomed in his dreams was a mortal animal and that they had departed for camp each November with no actual intention of slaying it because so far they had no actual hope of being able to. "We aint got the dog yet [Sam said]. It won't take but one. But he aint there. Maybe he aint nowhere." . . .

Twice while on stand during the next three years he [the boy] heard the dog strike its trail. Once he saw it cross a long corridor of down timber faster than he had ever believed it could have moved; he realised then why it would take a dog not only of abnormal courage but size and speed too ever to bring it to bay. He had a little dog at home, a mongrel, of the sort called fyce by negroes, a ratter, possessing that sort of courage which had long since stopped being bravery and had become foolhardiness. He brought it with him one June and himself and Sam Fathers with a brace of hounds on a rope leash lay downwind of the trail and actually ambushed the bear. They were so close that it turned at bay; it seemed to the boy that it would never stop rising, taller and taller, and even the two hounds seemed to have taken a kind of despairing courage from the fyce. Then he realized that the fyce was actually not going to stop. He flung the gun down and ran. When he overtook and grasped the shrill, frantically pinwheeling little dog, it seemed to him that he was directly under the bear. Then it was gone. Sam touched the little dog. "You's almost the one we wants," he said. "You just aint big enough. We aint got that one yet. He will need to be just a little bigger than smart, and a little braver than either."

It was in the fourth summer. Major de Spain's mare had foaled a horse colt. One evening the colt was missing. The next morning he [Sam] found the colt lying on its side, its throat torn out and the entrails and one ham partly eaten and no cat-mark, no claw-mark where a panther would have gripped it. Then on the third morning Sam led them to his little hut, to the corn-crib beyond it. He had removed the corn and had made a dead-fall of the door, baiting it with the colt's carcass; peering between the logs, they saw an animal almost the color of a gun or pistol barrel. It was not crouched nor even standing. It was in motion, in the air—a heavy body crashing with tremendous force against the door. "What in hell's name is it?" Major de Spain said.

"It's a dog," Sam said. "It's the dog."

"*The* dog?" Major de Spain said.

"That's gonter hold Old Ben."

"Dog the devil," Major de Spain said. "I'd rather have Old Ben himself in my pack than that brute. Shoot him."

"No," Sam said.

Each morning through the second week they would go to Sam's crib. Each morning they would watch him lower a pail of water into the crib while the dog hurled itself tirelessly against the door and dropped back and leaped again. It never made any sound and there was nothing frenzied in the act but only a cold and grim indomitable determination. Toward the end of the week it stopped jumping at the door. It was as if that time it simply disdained to jump any longer. It was not down. It stood, and they could see it now—part mastiff, something of Airedale and something of a dozen other strains probably, better than thirty inches at the shoulders and weighing as they guessed almost ninety pounds, with cold yellow eyes and a tremendous chest and over all that strange color like a blued gun-barrel.

They prepared to break camp. The boy begged to remain and he moved into the little hut with Sam Fathers. Each morning he watched Sam lower the pail of water into the crib. By the end of that week the dog was down. One morning it could not even reach the water. Sam took a short stick and prepared to enter the crib. It lay on its side while Sam touched it, the dog lying motionless, the yellow eyes open. There was in them a cold and almost impersonal malignance like some natural force.

"We dont want him tame," Boon said. "We want him like he is. We just want him to find out at last that the only way he can get out of that crib and stay out of it is to do what Sam or somebody tells him to do. He's the dog that's going to stop Old Ben and hold him. We've already named him. His name is Lion." . . .

It was December, the coldest December he had ever remembered. They had been in camp over two weeks, waiting for the weather to soften so that Lion and Old Ben could run their yearly race. Then he [the boy] was up, on the one-eyed mule which would not spook at wild blood, looking down at the dog motionless at Major de Spain's stirrup, looking in the grey streaming light bigger than a calf—the big head, the chest almost as big as his own, the blue hide beneath which the muscles flinched or quivered to no touch since the heart which drove the blood to them loved no man and no thing. They rode then.

He heard the changed note in the hounds' uproar and two hundred yards ahead he saw them. The bear had turned. He saw Lion drive in without pausing and saw the bear strike him aside and lunge into the yelling hounds and kill one of them almost in its tracks and whirl and run again. Then they were in a streaming tide of dogs. Then he and

Sam Fathers were riding alone. Boon was running along the edge of the bluff. He whirled and flung himself onto the mule behind the boy. They plunged down the bank and into the water. He got his leg over the mule as it came up out of the water. Boon grasped one stirrup as they went up the bank and crashed through the undergrowth and saw the bear, on its hind feet, its back against a tree while the bellowing hounds swirled around it and once more Lion drove in, leaping clear of the ground. This time the bear didn't strike him down. It caught the dog in both arms, almost loverlike, and they both went down. He was off the mule now. Boon was yelling something; he could see Lion still clinging to the bear's throat and he saw the bear, half erect, strike one of the hounds with one paw and hurl it five or six feet and then stand erect again and begin to rake at Lion's belly with its forepaws. Then Boon was running. The boy saw the gleam of the blade in his hand and watched him leap among the hounds and fling himself astride the bear, his legs locked around the bear's belly, his left arm under the bear's throat where Lion hung, and the glint of the knife as it rose and fell.

It fell just once. For an instant they almost resembled a piece of statuary: the clinging dog, the bear, the man astride its back, working and probing the buried blade. Then they went down, pulled over backward by Boon's weight, Boon underneath. The bear's back reappeared first, but Boon was astride it again. He had never released the knife and again the boy saw the almost infinitesimal movement of his arm and shoulder as he probed and sought; then the bear surged erect, and turned and still carrying the man and dog it took two or three steps toward the woods on its hind feet and crashed down. It didn't collapse, crumple. It fell all of a piece, as a tree falls, so all three of them, man dog and bear, seemed to bounce once.

He and Tennie's Jim ran forward. Boon was kneeling at the bear's head. Together they pried Lion's jaws from the bear's throat. "Easy, goddamn it," Boon said. "Can't you see his guts are all out of him?" Boon wrapped Lion in his hunting coat and carried him down to the skiff. "Come on, goddamn it!" he said. "Bring me that mule. I'm going to Hoke's to get the doctor. Can't you see his goddamn guts are all out of him?" They returned to camp through the streaming and sightless dark. Then they went on to the lighted house, the quiet faces as Boon entered, bloody and quite calm, carrying the bundled coat. He laid Lion, blood coat and all, on his stale sheetless pallet bed.

The sawmill doctor from Hoke's was already there. Boon would not let the doctor touch him until he had seen to Lion. He wouldn't risk giving Lion chloroform. He put the entrails back and sewed him up without it while Major de Spain held his head and Boon his feet. But he never tried to move. He lay there, the yellow eyes open upon nothing while the quiet men watched. Boon sat on the pallet bed with Lion's head under his hand. Then it was dawn and they all went out into the yard to look at Old Ben, with his eyes open too. Then Ash began to call them to breakfast and it was the first time he could remember hearing no sound from the dogs under the kitchen while they were eating. It was as if the old bear, even dead there in the yard, was a more potent terror still than they could face without Lion between them.

They moved Lion out to the front gallery, into the sun. It was Boon's idea. "Goddamn it," he said, "he never did want to stay in the house until I made him." He took a crowbar and loosened the floor boards under his pallet bed so it could be raised, mattress and all, without disturbing Lion's position, and they carried him out to the gallery and put him down facing the woods. And then they began to arrive, filling the little yard and overflowing it talking quietly of hunting, of the game and the dogs which ran it while from time to time the great blue dog would open his eyes, not as if he were listening to them but as though to look at the woods for a moment before closing his eyes again, to remember the woods or to see that they were still there. He died at sundown.

Major de Spain broke camp that night. They carried Lion into the woods, or Boon carried him that is, wrapped in a quilt from his bed, and the boy and General Compson and still almost fifty of them following with lanterns and lighted pine-knots. And Boon would let nobody else dig the grave either and lay Lion in it and cover him and then General Compson stood at the head of it while the blaze and smoke of the pine-knots streamed away among the winter branches and spoke as he would have spoken over a man.

JACK LONDON'S *Buck*

■ *In writing his well-known novel* The Call of the Wild, *London used his own experience in the Klondike gold rush of 1897 to portray authentically the law of club and fang that the dog Buck first endured and then adopted in order to survive. Buck's reversion to the wolfpack suggests the persistent atavism that London saw threatening the thin crust of civilization. In his later* White Fang, *however, he pictures a wolf-dog domesticated through human kindness.*

From THE CALL OF THE WILD

Buck lived at a big house in the sun-kissed Santa Clara Valley. And over this great demesne Buck ruled. There could not but be other dogs on so vast a place, but they did not count. The whole realm was his; he was king over all creeping, crawling, flying things of Judge Miller's place, humans included.

His father, Elmo, a huge St. Bernard, had been the Judge's inseparable companion, and Buck bid fair to follow in the way of his father. He was not so large,—he weighed only one hundred and forty pounds —for his mother, Shep, had been a Scotch shepherd dog. During the four years since his puppyhood he had lived the life of a sated aristocrat; he had a fine pride in himself, was even a trifle egotistical, as country gentlemen sometimes become. But he had saved himself by not becoming a mere pampered house dog. And this was the manner of dog Buck was in the fall of 1897, when the Klondike strike dragged men from all the world into the frozen North.

Buck did not know that Manuel, one of the gardener's helpers, was an undesirable acquaintance. No one saw him and Buck go off through the orchard on what Buck imagined was merely a stroll, and no one saw them arrive at the little flag station. Manuel doubled a piece of stout rope around Buck's neck under the collar. "Twist it, an' you'll choke 'em plentee," said Manuel, and the stranger grunted a ready affirmative.

Buck accepted the rope with quiet dignity. But to his surprise the rope tightened around his neck. In quick rage he sprang at the man, who grappled him close by the throat, and with a deft twist threw him over on his back. Then the rope tightened mercilessly, while Buck struggled in a fury. But his strength ebbed, his eyes glazed, and the two men threw him into the baggage car. Then the rope was removed, and he was flung into a cagelike crate and began a passage through many hands.

He was beaten (he knew that); but he was not broken. He saw, once and for all, that he stood no chance against a man with a club. It was his introduction to the reign of primitive law.

Buck's first day on the Dyea beach [an Alaskan village, starting point for the Klondike in the gold rush] was like a nightmare. He had been suddenly jerked from the heart of civilization and flung into the heart of things primordial. Here was neither peace, nor rest, nor a moment's safety. There was imperative need to be constantly alert; for these dogs and men were not town dogs and men. They were savages, all of them, who knew no law but the law of club and fang.

He had never seen dogs fight as these wolfish creatures fought, and his first experience taught him an unforgettable lesson. Curly was the victim. They were camped near the log store, where she, in her friendly way, made advances to a husky dog the size of a full-grown wolf, though not so large as she. There was no warning, only a leap in like a flash, a metallic clip of teeth, a leap out equally swift, and Curly's face was ripped open from eye to jaw. Thirty or forty huskies ran to the spot and surrounded the combatants in an intent and silent circle. Curly rushed her antagonist, who tumbled her off her feet. She never regained them. This was what the onlooking huskies had waited for. They closed in upon her, snarling and yelping, and she was buried, screaming with agony, beneath the bristling mass of bodies. . . .

Day after day, for days unending, Buck toiled in the traces. Always, they broke camp in the dark. And always they pitched camp after dark, eating their bit of fish, and crawling to sleep into the snow. Buck was ravenous. The pound and a half of sun-dried salmon, his ration for each day, seemed to go nowhere. He never had enough, and suffered from perpetual hunger pangs. He swiftly lost the fastidiousness which had characterized his old life. He watched and learned. When he saw Pike slyly steal a slice of bacon when Perrault's back was turned, he duplicated the performance the following day, getting away with the whole chunk. This first theft marked Buck as fit to survive in the hostile Northland environment. It marked his adaptability, the lack of which would have meant swift and terrible death. It marked, further, the decay of his moral nature, a vain thing and a handicap in the ruthless struggle for existence. And not only did he learn by experience but instincts long dead became alive again. The ancient song surged through him and he came into his own again.

Spitz, as lead-dog and acknowledged master of the team, felt his supremacy threatened by this strange Southland dog. It was inevitable that the clash for leadership should come. Buck wanted it because he had been gripped tight by that nameless, incomprehensible pride of the trail and trace—that pride which holds dogs in the toil to the last gasp, which lures them to die joyfully in the harness, and breaks their hearts if they are cut out of the harness. He openly threatened the other's leadership. He came between him and the shirks he should have punished. And he did it deliberately and craftily. With the covert mutiny of Buck, a general insubordination sprang up and increased. François, the dog-driver, was in constant apprehension of the life-and-death struggle he knew must take place sooner or later. . . .

In a flash Buck knew it. The time had come. Spitz was a practised fighter. In vain Buck strove to sink his teeth in the neck of the big white dog. Fang clashed fang, and lips were cut and bleeding, but Buck could not penetrate his enemy's guard. Spitz was untouched, while Buck was streaming with blood and panting hard. And all the while the silent and wolfish circle waited to finish off whichever dog went down. But Buck possessed a quality that made for greatness—imagination. He rushed, as though attempting the old shoulder trick, but at the last instant swept low to the snow and in. His teeth closed on Spitz's fore leg. There was a crunch of breaking bone, and the white dog faced him on three legs. He repeated the trick and broke the right fore leg. Spitz struggled madly to keep up. There was no hope for him. Buck was inexorable. Then Buck sprang in and out; shoulder had at last squarely met shoulder. The dark circle became a dot on the moon-flooded snow as Spitz disappeared from view. Buck stood and looked on, the successful champion, the dominant primordial beast who had made his kill and found it good. . . .

Buck was in open revolt. He wanted the leadership and would not be content with less. François grinned sheepishly at the courier, who shrugged his shoulders in sign they were beaten. The team stood harnessed to the sled in an unbroken line, ready for the trail. There was no place for Buck save at the front. Once more François called, and once more Buck laughed and kept away.

"T'row down de club," Perrault commanded.

François complied, whereupon Buck trotted in and swung around into position at the head of the team. His traces were fastened, the sled broken out, and they dashed out on to the river trail.

At a bound Buck took up the duties of leadership; and he showed himself the superior even of Spitz, of whom François had never seen an equal. But it was in giving the law and making his mates live up to it, that Buck excelled.

Thirty days from the time it left Dawson, the Salt Water Mail, with Buck and his mates at the fore, arrived at Skaguay. They were in a wretched state, worn out and worn down. Buck's one hundred and forty pounds had dwindled to one hundred and fifteen. Fresh batches of Hudson Bay dogs were to take the places of those worthless for the trail. Three days passed, by which time Buck and his mates found how really tired and weak they were. Then two men from the States [Hal and Charles] came along and bought them, harness and all, for a song. Buck felt vaguely that there was no depending on these two men and the woman. . . . Through it all Buck staggered along at the head of the team as in a nightmare. He pulled when he could; when he could no longer pull, he fell down and remained down till blows from whip or club drove him to his feet again.

It was beautiful spring weather, but neither dogs nor humans were aware of it. With the dogs falling, Mercedes [Charles's wife] weeping and riding, Hall swearing innocuously, and Charles's eyes wistfully watering, they staggered into John Thornton's camp at the mouth of the White River. When they halted, the dogs dropped down as though they had all been struck dead.

"Get up there, Buck! Mush on!" But the team did not get up at the command. The whip flashed out, here and there, on its merciless errands. John Thornton compressed his lips. Buck made no effort. He lay quietly where he had fallen. The lash bit into him again and again, but he neither whined nor struggled. He felt strangely numb. The last sensations of pain left him. And then, suddenly, without warning, uttering a cry that was inarticulate, John Thornton sprang upon the man who wielded the club. John Thornton stood over Buck, struggling to control himself. "If you strike that dog again, I'll kill you," he at last managed to say in a choking voice. "It's my dog," Hal replied. Thornton stood between him and Buck, and evinced no intention of getting out of the way. Hal drew his long hunting-knife. Thornton rapped Hal's knuckles with the axe-handle, knocking the knife to the ground. Then he stooped, picked it up himself, and with two strokes cut Buck's traces. Thornton knelt beside him and with rough, kindly hands searched for broken bones. John Thornton and Buck looked at each other. "You poor devil," said Thornton, and Buck licked his hand. . . .

Buck romped through his convalescence and into a new existence. Love, genuine passionate love, was his for the first time. Buck had a trick of love expression that was akin to hurt. He would often seize Thornton's hand in his mouth and close so fiercely that the flesh bore the impress of his teeth for some time afterward. For the most part, however, Buck's love was expressed in adoration. He would lie by the hour, eager, alert, at Thornton's feet, looking up into his face, dwelling upon it, studying it.

At Circle City, "Black" Burton, a man evil-tempered and malicious, had been picking a quarrel with a tenderfoot at the bar, when Thornton stepped good-naturedly between. Burton struck out, without warning, straight from the shoulder. Thornton was sent spinning. Those who were looking on heard what is best described as a roar, and they saw Buck's body rise up in the air as he left the floor for Burton's throat. The man saved his life by throwing out his arm, but Buck drove in again for the throat. This time the man succeeded only in partly blocking, and his throat was torn open. A "miner's meeting," called on the spot, decided the dog had sufficient provocation and his name spread through every camp in Alaska.

Spring came on once more, and at the end of all their wandering they found a shallow placer in a broad valley where gold showed like yellow butter. Buck spent long hours musing by the fire. Irresistible impulses seized him; especially he loved to run in the dim twilight of the summer midnights. One night he sprang from sleep with a start, eager-eyed, nostrils quivering and scenting, his mane bristling in recurrent waves. From the forest came the call, distinct and definite as never before,—a long-drawn howl, like, yet unlike, any noise made by husky dog. As he drew closer to the cry he came to an open place, and looking out saw with nose pointed to the sky, a long, lean, timber wolf.

He began to sleep out at night, staying away from camp for days at a time; and once he went down into the land of timber and streams. There he wandered for a week, killing his meat as he travelled. The blood-longing became stronger than ever before. He was a killer, surviving triumphantly in a hostile environment where only the strong survived. His cunning was a wolf-cunning and wild cunning; his intelligence, shepherd intelligence and St. Bernard intelligence. . . .

All day Buck brooded by the pool or roamed restlessly about the camp. From far away drifted a faint, sharp yelp, followed by a chorus of similar sharp yelps. Again Buck knew them as things heard in that other world which persisted in his memory. It was the call, the many-noted call, sounding more luringly and compelling than ever before. And as never before, he was ready to obey. John Thornton was dead [from an Indian raid]. The last tie was broken. Hunting their living meat the wolf pack had at last invaded Buck's valley. One wolf advanced cautiously and Buck recognized the wild brother with whom he had run for a night and a day. They touched noses. Then an old wolf, gaunt and battle-scarred, came forward. Buck writhed his lips with the preliminary of a snarl, but sniffed noses with him. Whereupon the old wolf sat down, pointed nose at the moon, and broke out the long wolf howl. The others sat back and howled. Buck, too, sat down and howled. The leaders lifted the yelp of the pack and sprang away into the woods. The wolves swung in behind. And Buck ran with them, side by side with the wild brother, yelping as he ran.

MARK TWAIN'S *Aileen*
Mavourneen

■ *Although "A Dog's Tale" (1904) is not one of Twain's literary gems,*
it embodies his consistent attitudes toward pretentiousness, family life,
injustice, and, above all, in his bitter later years his conviction that man
is the only animal that blushes—or needs to. It also sustains the protest
of Alexander Pope two centuries earlier against vivisectionists' indiffer-
ence to the suffering of the animals used in their experiments.

From A DOG'S TALE

My father was a St. Bernard, my mother was a collie, but I am a
Presbyterian. This is what my mother told me; I do not know these
nice distinctions myself. To me they are only fine large words meaning
nothing. My mother had a fondness for such; she liked to say them,
and see other dogs look surprised and envious. She got the words by
listening in the dining-room and drawing-room when there was company, and by going with the children to Sunday-school and listening
there; and whenever she heard a large word she said it over to herself
many times, and so was able to keep it until there was a dogmatic
gathering in the neighborhood, and then she could get it off and
surprise and distress them all. You can see that she was of a rather vain
and frivolous character; still, she had virtues, and enough to make up,
I think. She had a kind heart and gentle ways and she taught her
children her kindly way, and from her we learned also to be brave and

prompt in time of danger. And she taught us not by words only, but by example. Why, the brave things she did, you couldn't help admiring her, and you couldn't help imitating her. . . .

When I was well grown, at last, I was sold and taken away. She was broken-hearted, and so was I, but she comforted me as well as she could, and said we must do our duties without repining, [and] take our life [and] live it for the best good of others. She said men who did like this would have a noble and beautiful reward in another world, and although we animals would not go there, to do well and right would give to our brief lives a worthiness and dignity. And the last thing she said was, "In memory of me, when there is a time of danger to another, think of your mother and do as she would do." . . .

It was such a charming home—my new one; a fine great house, with spacious grounds around it, and the great garden. And I was the same as a member of the family; and they loved me, and did not give me a new name, but called me by my old one my mother had given me— Aileen Mavourneen. Mrs. Gray was thirty, and so sweet and so lovely, and Sadie was ten, and just like her mother, and the baby was a year old and fond of me, and never could get enough of hauling on my tail, and hugging me, and laughing out its innocent happiness; and Mr. Gray was thirty-eight, and tall and slender and handsome, businesslike, prompt, decided, unsentimental, and with that kind of trim-chisled face that just seems to glint and sparkle with frosty intellectuality! He was a renowned scientist. I do not know what the word means, but my mother would know how to use it and get effects.

Other times I lay on the floor in the mistress's work-room and slept, she gently using me for a foot-stool, knowing it pleased me, for it was a caress; other times I watched by the crib there, when the baby was asleep; other times I went visiting among the neighbor dogs—one very handsome and courteous and graceful, a curly-haired Irish setter by the name of Robin Adair, who was a Presbyterian like me, and belonged to the Scotch minister. By and by came my little puppy, and then my cup was full, my happiness was perfect. It was the dearest little wad-dling thing, and it made me so proud to see how the children and their mother adored it, and fondled it. It did seem to me that life was just too lovely to—

Then came the winter. One day I was standing a watch in the nursery. The baby was asleep in the crib, the kind of crib that has a lofty tent over it made of gauzy stuff. A spark from the wood-fire shot out, and lit on the slope of the tent. A scream from the baby woke me, and there was that tent flaming up toward the ceiling! Before I could think, I sprang to the floor in my fright, and in a second was half-way to the door; but the next half-second my mother's farewell was sounding in my ears, and I was back on the bed again. I reached my head through the flames and dragged the baby out by the waist-band, and tugged it along, and we fell to the floor together in a cloud of smoke; I snatched a new hold, and dragged the screaming little creature along and out at the door and around the bend of the hall, and was still tugging away, all excited and happy and proud, when the master's voice shouted: "Begone, you cursed beast!" and I jumped to save myself; but he chased me, striking furiously at me with his cane, I dodging this way and that, in terror; and at last a strong blow fell upon my left foreleg; the cane went up for another blow, but never descended, for the nurse's voice rang wildly out, "The nursery's on fire!" and the master rushed away in that direction.

The pain was cruel, but I limped on three legs to the other end of the hall, where there was a dark little stairway leading up into a garret where people seldom went. I managed to climb up there, then I hid in the secretest place I could find. For half an hour there was a commotion downstairs, and shoutings, and rushing footsteps, and then there was quiet again. Then came a sound that froze me. They were calling me—calling me by name—hunting for me!

They called and called—days and nights. So long that the hunger and thirst near drove me mad, and I recognized that I was getting very weak. Once I woke in an awful fright—it seemed to me that the calling was right there in the garret! And so it was: it was Sadie's voice, and she was crying; and I could not believe my ears for the joy of it when I heard her say: "Come back to us—oh, come back to us, and forgive —." I broke in with *such* a grateful little yelp, and the next moment Sadie was plunging through the darkness and shouting, "She's found, she's found!"

The days that followed—well, they were wonderful. The mother and Sadie and the servants—why, they just seemed to worship me. Every day the friends and neighbors flocked in to hear about my heroism and a dozen times a day Mrs. Gray and Sadie would tell the tale to newcomers. And when the people wanted to know what made me limp, they looked ashamed and changed the subject.

And this was not all the glory; no, the master's friends came and discussed me as if I was a kind of discovery; and some of them said it was wonderful in a dumb beast, the finest exhibition of instinct they could call to mind; but the master said, with vehemence, "It's far above instinct; it's *reason,* and many a man, has less of it than this poor silly quadruped that's foreordained to perish"; and then he laughed, and said: "Why, look at me—with all my grand intelligence, the only thing I inferred was that the dog had gone mad and was destroying the child, whereas but for the beast's intelligence, the child would have perished!" Then they discussed optics, as they called it, and whether a certain injury to the brain would produce blindness or not, but they could not agree about it, and said they must test it by experiment by and by; and next they discussed plants, and that interested me, because in the summer Sadie and I had planted seeds—I helped her dig the holes and after days and days a little shrub or flower came up there.

Pretty soon it was spring, and sunny and pleasant and lovely, and the sweet mother and children patted me and the puppy good-by, and went away on a journey and a visit to their kin. And one day those men came again, and said, now for the test, and they took the puppy to the laboratory, and I limped three-leggedly along, feeling proud, for any attention shown the puppy was a pleasure to me, of course. They discussed and experimented, and then suddenly the puppy shrieked, and they set him on the floor, and he went staggering around, with his head all bloody, and the master clapped his hands and shouted: "There, I've won—confess it! He's blind as a bat!" And they all said —"you've proved your theory," and praised him.

But I hardly saw or heard those things, for I ran at once to my little darling, and licked the blood, and it put its head against mine, and I knew in my heart it was a comfort to it in its pain and trouble to feel its mother's touch, though it could not see me. Then it dropped down presently, and its little velvet nose rested upon the floor, and it was still.

Soon the master stopped discussing a moment, and rang in the footman, and said, "Bury it in the far corner of the garden," and then went on with the discussion, and I trotted along after the footman, very happy and grateful, for I knew the puppy was out of its pain now, because it was asleep. We went far down the garden, where the children and the nurse and the puppy and I used to play, and there the footman dug a hole, and I saw he was going to plant the puppy, and I was glad, because it would grow and come up a fine handsome dog, like Robin Adair, and be a beautiful surprise for the family when they came home. When the footman had finished and covered little Robin up, he patted my head, and there were tears in his eyes, and he said: "Poor little doggie, you SAVED *his* child."

I have watched two whole weeks, and he doesn't come up! This last week a fright has been stealing upon me. I do not know what it is, but the fear makes me sick, and I cannot eat, though the servants bring me the best of food; and they pet me so, and even come in the night, and cry, and say, "Poor doggie—do give it up and come home; *don't* break our hearts!" And I am so weak; since yesterday I cannot stand on my feet anymore. And within this hour the servants looking toward the sun where it was sinking out of sight and the night chill coming on, said things I could not understand, but they carried something cold to my heart.

"Those poor creatures! They do not suspect. They will come home in the morning, and eagerly ask for the little doggie that did the brave deed, and who of us will be strong enough to say the truth to them: 'The humble little friend is gone where go the beasts that perish.'"

ANNA HEMPSTEAD BRANCH'S *Dog*

■ *As a well-known American poet in the first part of this century, Anna Hempstead Branch tended to deal with humanitarian and metaphysical themes. In this poem she rejects the Christian and Cartesian dualism which denied souls to dogs. Perhaps under the influence of Darwinism and Transcendentalism she perceived in canine behavior moral impulses which ultimately derive from the same spiritual sources that underlie human virtues.*

TO A DOG
(Sections I and II)

I

If there is no God for thee
Then there is no God for me,

If He sees not when you share
With the poor your frugal fare,

Does not see you at a grave,
Every instinct bred to save;

As if you were the only one
Believing in a resurrection;

When you wait, as lovers do,
Watching till your friend comes true;

Does not reverence when you take
Angry words for love's sweet sake;

If his eye does not approve
All your faith and pain and love;

If the heart of justice fail
And is for you of no avail;

If there is no heaven for thee
Then there is no heaven for me.

II

If the Lord they tell us of
Died for men yet loves not love,

If from out His Paradise
He shuts the innocent and wise,

The gay, obedient, simple, good,
The docile ones, of friendly mood,

Those who die to save a friend
Heavenly faithful to the end;

If there is no cross for thee
Then there is no cross for me.

■ *Of the many dogs of varied breeds which the Galsworthys cared for over the years, the deepest mutual attraction lay between them and a spaniel named Chris, acquired in 1906. (He was sometimes called John because the dog John in Galsworthy's* Country House, *written the next year, was closely modeled on Chris.) Chris's early death at Christmas in 1911 had a profound effect upon both Galsworthys, evoking from the novelist an absorbing account of his character and behavior in "Memories," and from Ada a traumatic experience of having a visitation from him after his death. Like Scott, Galsworthy did much of his writing with a dog by his chair. In view of the Galsworthys' devotion to Chris it may seem odd that his name is never mentioned in "Memories." Apparently Galsworthy wished to depersonalize him and make him an archetype of what in the essay he calls "dog." This depersonalization extends to himself and his wife. That Chris' life and character were reflected in "Memories" is convincingly shown in a biography of Galsworthy,* The Man of Principle, *by Dudley Barker.*

From MEMORIES

We set out to meet him at Waterloo Station—I, who had owned his impetuous mother, knowing a little what to expect, while to my companion he would be all original. We stood there waiting, and wondering what sort of new thread Life was going to twine into our skein.

From behind a wooden crate we saw a long black muzzled nose poking round at us. We took him out—soft, wobbly, tearful; set him down on his four, as yet not quite simultaneous legs, and regarded him.

He wandered a little round our legs, neither wagging his tail nor licking at our hands; then he looked up, and my companion said: "He's an angel!"

And just then something must have stirred in him, for he turned up his swollen nose and stared at my companion, and a little later rubbed the dry pinkness of his tongue against my thumb. In that look, and that unconscious restless lick, he was trying hard to leave unhappiness behind, trying hard to feel that these new creatures with stroking paws and queer scents, were his mother; yet all the time he knew, I am sure, that they were something bigger, more permanently, desperately, his. The first sense of being owned, perhaps (who knows) of owning, had stirred in him. He would never again be quite the same unconscious creature.

A little way from the end of our journey we got out and dismissed the cab. He could not too soon know the scents and pavements of this London where the chief of his life must pass. I can see now his first bumble down that wide, back-water of a street, how continually and suddenly he sat down to make sure of his own legs, how continually he lost our heels. He showed us then in full perfection what was afterwards to be an inconvenient—if enduring—characteristic: At any call or whistle he would look in precisely the opposite direction.

That night, indeed, for several nights, he slept with me, keeping me too warm down my back, and waking me now and then with quaint sleepy whimperings. Indeed, all through his life he flew a good deal in his sleep, fighting dogs and seeing ghosts, running after rabbits and thrown sticks; and to the last one never quite knew whether or no to rouse him when his four black feet began to jerk and quiver. His dreams were like our dreams, both good and bad; happy sometimes, sometimes tragic to weeping point.

He ceased to sleep with me the day we discovered that he was a perfect little colony, whose settlers were of an active species which I have never seen again. He would sleep anywhere, so long as it was in [our] room, or so close outside it as to make no matter, for it was with him a principle that what he did not smell did not exist. I would I could hear again those long rubber-lipped snufflings of recognition underneath the door, with which each morning he would regale and reassure a spirit that grew with age more and more nervous and delicate about this matter of propinquity! For he was a dog of fixed ideas, things stamped on his mind were indelible; as, for example, his duty towards cats, for whom he had really a perverse affection, which had led to that first disastrous moment of his life, when he was brought up, poor bewildered puppy, from a brief excursion to the kitchen, with one eye closed and his cheek torn! He bore to his grave that jagged scratch across the eye. It was in dread of a repetition of this tragedy that he was instructed at the word "Cats" to rush forward with a special "tow-row-rowing," which he never used towards any other form of creature. To the end he cherished a hope that he would reach the cat, but never did; and if he had, we knew he would only have stood and wagged his tail.

His eye and nose were impeccable in their sense of form; indeed, he was very English in that matter: People must be just so; things smell properly; and affairs go on in the one right way. He could tolerate neither creatures in ragged clothes, nor children on their hands and knees, nor postmen, because, with their bags, they swelled-up on one side, and carried lanterns on their stomachs. He would never let the harmless creatures pass without religious barks. Naturally a believer in authority and routine, and distrusting spiritual adventure, he yet had curious fads that seemed to have nested in him, quite outside of all principle. He would, for instance, follow neither carriages nor horses, and if we tried to make him, at once left for home, where he would sit with nose raised to Heaven, emitting through it a most lugubrious, shrill noise. Then again, one must not place a stick, a slipper, a glove, or anything with which he could play, upon one's head—since such an action reduced him at once to frenzy. For so conservative a dog, his environment was sadly anarchistic. He never complained in words of our shifting habits, but curled his head round over his left paw and pressed his chin very hard against the ground whenever he smelled packing. What necessity,—he seemed continually to be saying,—what real necessity is there for change of any kind whatever? Here we were all together, and one day was like another, so that I knew where I was —and now *you* only know what will happen next; and *I*—I can't tell you whether I shall be with you when it happens! What strange, grieving minutes a dog passes at such times in the underground of his subconsciousness, refusing realisation, yet all the time only too well divining. Some careless word, some unmuted compassion in voice, the stealthy wrapping of a pair of boots, the unaccustomed shutting of a door that ought to be open, the removal from a down-stair room of an object always there—one tiny thing, and he knows for certain that he is not going too. He fights against the knowledge just as we do against what we cannot bear; he gives up hope, but not effort, protesting in the only way he knows of, and now and then heaving a great sigh. Those sighs of a dog! They go to the heart so much more deeply than the sighs of our own kind, because they are utterly unintended, regardless of effect, emerging from one who, heaving them, knows not that they have escaped him!

The words: "Yes—going too!" spoken in a certain tone, would call up in his eyes a still-questioning half-happiness, and from his tail a quiet flutter, but did not quite serve to put to rest either his doubt or his feeling that it was all unnecessary—until the cab arrived. Then he would pour himself out of door or window, and be found in the bottom of the vehicle, looking severely away from an admiring cabman. Once settled on our feet he travelled with philosophy, but no digestion.

Each August, till he was six, he was sent for health, and the assuagement of his hereditary instincts, up to a Scotch shooting, where he carried many birds in a very tender manner. Once he was compelled by Fate to remain there nearly a year; and we went up ourselves to fetch him home. Down the long avenue towards the keeper's cottage we walked. We approached him silently. Suddenly his nose went up from its imagined trail, and he came rushing at our legs. From him, as a garment drops from a man, dropped all his strange soberness; he became in a single instant one fluttering eagerness. He leaped from life to life in one bound, without hesitation, without regret. Not one sigh, not one look back, not the faintest token of gratitude or regret at leaving those good people who had tended him for a whole year, buttered oat-cake for him, allowed him to choose each night exactly where he would sleep. No, he just marched out beside us, as close as ever he could get, drawing us on in spirit, and not even attending to the scents, until the lodge gates were passed. They tell me he developed a lovely nose and perfect mouth, large enough to hold gingerly the biggest hare. I well believe it, remembering the qualities of his mother, whose character, however, in stability he far surpassed. But, as *he* grew every year more devoted to dead grouse and birds and rabbits, *I* liked them more and more alive; it was the only real breach between us, and we kept it out of sight.

The call of the wild—Spring running—whatever it is—that besets men and dogs, seldom attained full mastery over him; but one could often see it struggling against his devotion to the scent of us, and, watching that dumb contest, I have time and again wondered how far this civilisation of ours was justifiably imposed on him; how far the love for us that we had so carefully implanted could ever replace in him the satisfaction of his primitive wild yearnings. He was like a man, naturally polygamous, married to one loved woman. It was surely not for nothing that Rover is dog's most common name, and would be ours, but for our too tenacious fear of losing something, to admit, even to ourselves, that we are hankering.

The history of his one wandering, for which no respectable reason can be assigned, will never, of course, be known. It was in London, of an October evening, when we were told he had slipped out and was not anywhere. Then began those four distressful hours of searching for that black needle in that blacker bundle of hay. Hours of real dismay and suffering—for it is suffering, indeed, to feel a loved thing swallowed up in that hopeless maze of London streets. Stolen or run over? Which was worst? The neighbouring police stations visited, the Dog's Home notified, an order for five hundred "Lost Dog" bills placed in the printer's hands, the streets patrolled! And then, in a lull snatched for food, and still endeavouring to preserve some aspect of assurance, we heard the bark which meant: "Here is a door I cannot open!" We hurried forth, and there he was on the top doorstep—busy, unashamed, giving no explanations, asking for his supper; and very shortly after him came his five hundred "Lost Dog" bills.

Ah! and there was that other time, when it was reported to me, returning home at night, that he had gone out to find me; and I went forth again, disturbed, and whistling his special call to the empty fields. Suddenly out of the darkness I heard a rushing, and he came furiously dashing against my heels from he alone knew where he had been lurking and saying to himself: I will not go in till he comes! I could not scold, there was something too lyrical in the return of that live, lonely, rushing piece of blackness through the blacker night. He was not a "clever" dog; and guiltless of all tricks. Nor was he ever "shown." We did not even dream of subjecting him to this indignity. Was our dog a clown, a hobby, a fad, a fashion, a feather in our caps—that we should subject him to periodic pennings in stuffy halls, that we should harry his faithful soul with such tomfoolery? He never even heard us talk about his lineage, deplore the length of his nose, or call him "clever-looking." We should have been ashamed to let him smell about us the tar-brush of a sense of property, to let him think we looked on him as an asset to earn us pelf or glory. We wished that there should be between us the spirit that was between the sheep-dog and that farmer, who, when asked his dog's age, touched the old creature's head, and answered thus: "Teresa" (his daughter) "was born in November, and this one in August." That sheep-dog had seen eighteen years when the great white day came for him, and his spirit passed away up, to cling with the wood-smoke round the dark rafters of the kitchen where he had lain so vast a time beside his master's boots. No, no! If a man does not soon pass beyond the thought: "By what shall this dog profit me?" into the large state of simple gladness to be with dog, he shall never know the very essence of that companionship which depends not on the points of dog, but on some strange and subtle mingling of mute spirits. For it is by muteness that a dog becomes for one so utterly beyond value; with him one is at peace, where words play no torturing tricks.

He did not at all mind one's being absorbed in other humans; he seemed to enjoy the sounds of conversation lifting round him, and to know when they were sensible. He could not, for instance, stand actors or actresses giving readings of their parts, perceiving at once that the same had no connection with the minds and real feelings of the speakers; and, having wandered a little to show his disapproval, he would go to the door and stare at it till it opened and let him out. Once or twice, it is true, when an actor of large voice was declaiming an emotional passage, he so far relented as to go up to him and pant in his face. Music, too, made him restless, inclined to sigh, and to ask questions. Sometimes, at its first sound, he would cross to the window and remain there looking for Her. At other, he would simply go and lie on the loud pedal, and we never could tell whether it was from sentiment, or because he thought that in this way he heard less. At one special Nocturne of Chopin's he always whimpered. He *was*, indeed, of rather Polish temperament—very gay when he was gay, dark and brooding when he was not.

Nor was he a fighting dog; but once attacked, he lacked a sense of values, being unable to distinguish between dogs that he could beat and dogs with whom he had "no earthly." It was, in fact, as well to interfere at once, especially in the matter of retrievers, for he never forgot having in his youth been attacked by a retriever from behind. No, he never forgot, and never forgave, an enemy. Only a month before that day of which I cannot speak, being very old and ill, he engaged an Irish terrier on whose impudence he had long had his eye, and routed him.

And how a battle cheered his spirit! He was certainly no Christian; but, allowing for essential dog, he was very much a gentleman. And I do think that most of us who live on this earth these days would rather leave it with that label on us than the other. For to be a Christian, as Tolstoy understood the word—and no one else in our time has had logic and love of truth enough to give it coherent meaning—is (to be quite sincere) not suited to men of Western blood. Whereas—to be a gentleman! It is a far cry, but perhaps it can be done. In him, at all events, there was no pettiness, no meanness, and no cruelty, and though he fell below his ideal at times, this never altered the true look of his eyes, nor the simple loyalty in his soul.

But what a crowd of memories come back, bringing with them the perfume of fallen days! What delights and glamour, what long hours of effort, discouragements, and secret fears did he not watch over—our black familiar; and with the sight and scent and touch of him, deepen or assuage! How many thousand walks did we not go together, so that we still turn to see if he is following at his padding gait, attentive to the invisible trails. Not the least hard thing to bear when they go from us, these quiet friends, is that they carry away with them so many years of our own lives. Yet, if they find warmth therein, who would grudge them those years that they have so guarded? Nothing else of us can they take to lie upon with outstretched paws and chin pressed to the ground; and, whatever they take, be sure they have deserved.

Do they know, as we do, that their time must come? Yes, they know, at rare moments. No other way can I interpret those pauses of his latter life, when, propped on his forefeet, he would sit for long minutes quite motionless—his head drooped, utterly withdrawn; then turn those eyes of his and look at me. That look said more plainly than all words could: "Yes, I know that I must go!" If *we* have spirits that persist—*they* have. If *we* know after our departure, who we were—*they* do. No one, I think, who really longs for truth, can ever glibly say which it will be for dog and man—persistence or extinction of our consciousness. There is but one thing certain—the childishness of fretting over that eternal question. Whichever it be, it must be right, the only possible thing. He felt that too, I know; but then, like his master, he was what is called a pessimist.

My companion tells me that, since he left us, he has once come back. It was Old Year's Night, and she was sad, when he came to her in visible shape of his black body, passing round the dining-table from the window-end, to his proper place beneath the table, at her feet. She saw him quite clearly; she heard the padding tap-tap of his paws and very toe-nails; she felt his warmth brushing hard against the front of her skirt. She thought then that he would settle down upon her feet, but something disturbed him, and he stood pausing, pressed against her, then moved out towards where I generally sit, but was not sitting that night. She saw him stand there, as if considering; then at some sound or laugh, she became self-conscious, and slowly, very slowly, he was no longer there. Had he some message, some counsel to give, something he would say, that last night of the last year of all those he had watched over us? Will he come back again?

No stone stands over where he lies. It is on our hearts that his life is engraved.

EDGAR LEE MASTERS' *Nig*

■ *In the cemetery of the small fictional Midwestern town of Spoon River, Edgar Lee Masters imagines the self-revelatory epitaphs of over two hundred of the deceased as they might have written them. In "Benjamin Pantier" Pantier explains his failure to cope with the worldly ways of a predatory society, which includes his wife. As Byron found in Boatswain, a century earlier, a striking canine antithesis to the hypocrisy and injustice underlying social and political eminence, so Pantier discovered that only his dog remained as solace and trustworthy friend. (In an adjoining epitaph in* Spoon River Anthology *Mrs. Pantier presents her version of her husband's disintegration.)*

BENJAMIN PANTIER

Together in this grave lie Benjamin Pantier, attorney at law,
And Nig, his dog, constant companion, solace and friend.
Down the gray road, friends, children, men and women,
Passing one by one out of life, left me till I was alone
With Nig for partner, bed-fellow, comrade in drink.
In the morning of life I knew aspiration and saw glory.
Then she, who survives me, snared my soul
With a snare which bled me to death,
Till I, once strong of will, lay broken, indifferent,
Living with Nig in a room back of a dingy office.
Under my jaw-bone is snuggled the bony nose of Nig—
Our story is lost in silence. Go by, mad world!

HAROLD MONRO'S *Dog*

■ *One of the major figures in the Georgian revolt in English poetry in the first quarter of this century, Monro established the Poetry Bookshop with the hope of creating a wide public taste for poetry, in part by treating subjects close to everyday life. In "Dog," one of his most memorable poems, he is especially adept at projecting the dog's feelings and sensations.*

DOG

You little friend, your nose is ready; you sniff,
Asking for that expected walk,
(Your nostrils full of the happy rabbit-whiff)
And almost talk.

And so the moment becomes a moving force;
Coats glide down from their pegs in the humble dark;
The sticks grow live to the stride of their vagrant course.
You scamper the stairs,
Your body informed with the scent and the track and the mark
Of stoats and weasels, moles and badgers and hares.

We are going *out*. You know the pitch of the word,
Probing the tone of thought as it comes through fog
And reaches by devious means (half-smelt, half-heard)
The four-legged brain of a walk-ecstatic dog.

Out in the garden your head is already low.
(Can you smell the rose? Ah, no.)
But your limbs can draw
Life from the earth through the touch of your padded paw.

Now, sending a little look to us behind,
Who follow slowly the track of your lovely play,
You carry our bodies forward away from mind
Into the light and fun of your useless day.

* * *

Thus, for your walk, we took ourselves, and went
Out by the hedge and the tree to the open ground.
You ran, in delightful strata of wafted scent,
Over the hill without seeing the view;
Beauty is smell upon primitive smell to you:
To you, as to us, it is distant and rarely found.

Home . . . and further joy will be surely there:
Supper waiting full of the taste of bone.
You throw up your nose again, and sniff, and stare
For the rapture known
Of the quick wild gorge of food and the still lie-down
While your people talk above you in the light
Of candles, and your dreams will merge and drown
Into the bed-delicious hours of night.

CARL SANDBURG'S *Dan*

■ *Although allusions to animals are not prominent in Sandburg's poems or stories, he was at least familiar enough with dogs to note in* The People, Yes *that a dog's nose is one of the three coldest objects. In "Dan" (1920) he paints with evident precision, fondness, and economy what is essentially a canine still life of a dozing pup. The configuration, blended coloration, and distinctive setting could readily be transposed to canvas by a Sir Edwin Landseer.*

DAN

Early May, after cold rain the sun
        baffling cold wind.
Irish setter pup finds a corner near
        the cellar door, all sun and no wind,
Cuddling there he crosses forepaws
        and lays his skull
Sideways on this pillow, dozing in
        a half-sleep,
Browns of hazel nut, mahogany, rosewood, played off
        against each other on his paws and head.

Mickey

■ *Although the late Loren Eiseley was professionally known as a distin-guished anthropologist and archaeologist, he recognized the fallibility of a purely scientific approach. His ultimate concerns were broadly humanis-tic—not only the cave dwellers' emergence from darkness but also the aspirations of canines like Mickey for a higher level of civilized maturity. Indeed, in the final pages of his autobiography* All the Strange Hours, *Eiseley refers several times to his own dog Wolf and says, "I think we dreamed the same dreams, that dog and I." Much of his writing is autobio-graphical and reflects fresh insights of the imagination and the persistence of mystery in the animate world.*

From PAW MARKS AND BURIED TOWNS

Many years ago, when the first cement sidewalks were being laid in our neighborhood, we children took the paw of our dog Mickey and impressed it into a kind of immortality even as he modestly floundered and objected. Some time ago after the lapse of many decades, I stood and looked at the walk, now crumbling at the edges from the feet of many passers. No one knows where Mickey the friendly lies; no one knows how many times the dust that clothed that beautiful and loving spirit has moved with the thistledown across the yards where Mickey used to play. Here is his only legacy to the future—that dabbled paw mark whose secret is remembered briefly in the heart of an aging professor.

The mark of Mickey's paw is dearer to me than many more impressive monuments—perhaps because, in a sense, we both wanted to be something other than what we were. Mickey, I know, wanted very much to be a genuine human being. If permitted, he would sit up to the table and put his paws together before his plate, like the rest of the children. If anyone mocked him at such a time by pretending to have paws and resting his chin on the table as Mickey had to do, Mickey would growl and lift his lip. He knew very well he was being mocked for not being human. The reminder that he was only a poor dog with paws annoyed Mickey. He knew a lot more than he ever had the opportunity to express. Though people refused to take Mickey's ambition seriously, the frustration never affected his temperament. Being of a philosophic cast of mind, he knew that children were less severe in their classifications. And if Mickey found the social restrictions too onerous to enable him quite to achieve recognition inside the house, outside he came very close to being a small boy. In fact, he was taken into a secret order we had founded whose club house was an old piano box in the backyard. We children never let the fact that Mickey walked on four legs blind us to his other virtues.

Now the moral to this is that Mickey tried hard to be a human being. And as I stood after the lapse of years and looked at the faint impression of his paw, it struck me that every ruined civilization is, in a sense, the mark of men trying to be human, trying to transcend themselves. Like Mickey, none of them has quite made it, but they have each left a figurative paw mark—the Shang bronzes, the dreaming stone faces on Easter Island, the Parthenon, the Sphinx. The North African cities of Sabratha and Leptis Magna, remnants of Roman civilization, once as powerful as our own, are dissolving under sand and wind. Now the theaters lie empty and open to the sun; but still the bold Roman letters stand across the entrance to the theater at Leptis Magna, naming, amid the surrounding ruin, one Annobal, the donor. Annobal has left a paw mark and gone thence, like my dog Mickey.

■ *The concern that Hardy felt over injustice and destructive fate in the human world he extended to the lives of animals. He was especially distressed by the abuse of horses and the massive slaughter of birds. On the grounds of Max Gate, his residence, there was a pet cemetery where cats and his two dogs were buried: Moss (beaten to death by a tramp) and Wessex, described on his stone as a "famous dog," "faithful," and "unflinching." Dogs are the subject of several of Hardy's poems and also appear in his fiction set in the Wessex countryside. Generally they suffer from human callousness. Hardy's equation would seem to be: As men and women like Tess of the D'Urbervilles are victims of "the sport" of the "President of the Immortals," dogs are pawns in the sport of men.*

THE MONGREL

In Havenpool Harbour the ebb was strong,
And a man with a dog drew near and hung,
And taxpaying day was coming along,
    So the mongrel had to be drowned.
The man threw a stick from the paved wharf-side
Into the midst of the ebbing tide,
And the dog jumped after with ardent pride
    To bring the stick aground.

But no: the steady suck of the flood
To seaward needed, to be withstood,
More than the strength of mongrelhood
    To fight its treacherous trend.
So, swimming for life with desperate will,
The struggler with all his natant skill
Kept buoyant in front of his master, still
    There standing to wait the end.

The loving eyes of the dog inclined
To the man he held as a god enshrined,
With no suspicion in his mind
    That this had all been meant.
Till the effort not to drift from shore
Of his little legs grew slower and slower,
And, the tide still outing with brookless power,
    Outward the dog, too, went.

Just ere his sinking what does one see
Break on the face of that devotee?
A wakening to the treachery
    He had loved with love so blind?
The faith that had shone in that mongrel's eye
That his owner would save him by and by
Turned to much like a curse as he sank to die,
    And a loathing of mankind.

IRENE RUTHERFORD McLEOD'S *Lone Dog*

■ *Irene McLeod (Mrs. Aubrey De Selincourt), apparently a widely read English poet in the early decades of this century, was avowedly concerned with creating a society where love and justice prevail. In* Songs to Save a Soul *she included portraits of outcasts or rebels like the lone dog who quested for a less complacent and constricting milieu.*

LONE DOG

I'm a lean dog, a keen dog, a wild dog, and lone:
I'm a rough dog, a tough dog, hunting on my own:
I'm a bad dog, a mad dog, teasing silly sheep:
I love to sit and bay the moon, to keep fat souls from sleep.

I'll never be a lap dog, licking dirty feet,
A sleek dog, a meek dog, cringing for my meat—
Not for me the fireside, the well-filled plate,
But shut door, and sharp stone, and cuff and kick, and hate.

Not for me the other dogs, running by my side:
Some have run a short while, but none of them would bide.
O mine is still the lone trail, the hard trail, the best,
Wide wind, and wild stars, and hunger of the quest!

ADMIRAL RICHARD BYRD'S *Huskies*

■ *In* By Dog Sled for Byrd, *his account of the traversal of sixteen hundred miles of antarctic ice on dog sled as a surveyor in the Byrd expedition, John S. O'Brien has provided a comprehensive portrait of the husky breed. Repeatedly the huskies exhibit not only their eagerness, instinctive skill, and endurance but also their devotion to the drivers of their sled. Several of the dogs are accorded individual profiles for their essentially heroic conduct—notably Lady, Tickle, and Dinty. O'Brien wrote several other books on the huskies including* Silver Chief, Dog of the North *and* Valiant, Dog of the Timberline.

From BY DOG SLED FOR BYRD

Tension is high. For this is just twenty minutes after one on the afternoon of November 4, 1929, and within the next few minutes one of the most remarkable journeys on record will begin. For over a year we forty-two men have lived together; together we have built our base camp, Little America, doing the hard preparatory work that must precede any trip into the Antarctic wastes. See the dogs! Even they sense the unusual. Not a sound do they make, but with ears alertly cocked, and shining eyes, they follow every move. There goes Norman Vaughan after his leader, Dinty. And that is a signal for the rest. Instantly all the huskies break into such a chorus of barking and howling that one can scarcely make himself heard. It takes stout ropes and deeply driven stakes to hold the anxious dogs from dashing off helter-skelter today. The anchor ropes are jerked loose, the men holding the dogs leap back. No command is needed, for with one jump the dogs are away, snow flying in clouds from their racing feet.

Once upon the bay we are confronted by Antarctic's most dreaded weapon—blizzard. With long open leads of water on all sides, half-blinded by the flying snow, swerving, skidding, dodging, we swing along at a racing speed. The dogs respond to our shouts of "gee" and "haw," but their animal sense of danger is far keener than our ability to direct them. Time and again, of their own accord they swerve sharply aside with breathtaking suddenness, escaping by a few inches some huge crack in the ice through which the oily sea water is lapping hungrily for us. Without their instinctive knowledge of danger we might have steered directly into those cracks.

Picketing of the dogs is one of the most important problems confronting men on the trail. The dogs must at all times be secure—not only because they fight to the death if they gain their freedom; but also because they will eat not only food, but harness and lashings as well. Many expeditions have been seriously crippled because the dogs got loose and went on a rampage of maiming each other in wild fights, and then topping off the performance with a light lunch of lashes and harness.

The lines out, we now put the dogs "to bed." Each in his turn is taken to his place on the picket line. Feeding comes next. Each driver takes out enough pound-and-a-half cakes of pemmican for his team. One by one they give their chops a few licks, nose around for any crumbs, and then do their regular two or three turns before lying down on the cold, hard snow for a well-earned rest. . . .

But those animals! They certainly were the world's champion dogs. They had shaken off the covering of snow that had been whirled on them by the wind during the night and were ready to start. Most of them had taken a few bites of snow, which is a husky's idea of a drink. But we could never cure them of that mad start every morning that tangled them into a fighting mass. Such a snarling, biting mass of fur and fangs as they were!

Blizzard, leader of Goodale's team, was a one-man dog. Typical gray husky, he allowed anyone to pet him but showed no enthusiasm for anybody but Ed. In Norm's team we had a pretty little mother dog named Lady. We all made a business of showing her we were her friends, and she grew to trust us. During the past winter, when it was sixty below zero, she brought six beautiful little huskies into the world. No human mother could have showered more love and attention on her children than Lady did. When we left for the trail, it was hard to take Lady from her babies. She was thin and whimpered a lot and was terribly lonesome for her pups. She was paired with an old fellow who grew annoyed with her whimpering and barking. But with all her whimpering, Lady was a thoroughbred, pulling as hard as any dog in camp. But at last she dropped, and although we lashed her on a sledge and let her rest and ride, we had to lose her in the end.

My leader, Pete, was a fine dog. When he would come and lay his head on my knee and look up into my eyes, I could feel the love and faith he could not put into words. Then there were the Siberian twins, Oomiyak and Kayak. They were the gentlest, most lovable dogs of the entire pack, and faithful hard workers. When I would bend over to take one of them from the picket line, the other would put a paw gently against my knee as if to say, "I don't want to disturb you, but how about a little petting?" Of all the dogs in my team I loved them best, for they had characters many a human being might envy. The wheel team next to my sledge was the snow white Dingo and his running mate, jet black Targish. Biggest and strongest in the pack, they had the most remarkable strength I have ever seen. On more than one occasion those two started off by themselves to pull the entire load of a thousand or twelve hundred pounds. Quimbo was mostly black, with brown markings on his face. Although very friendly, he did not seek attention and was decidedly dignified in behavior. But the twins that were stabled next to him, Dolph and Cito, never could get enough petting. These two gray and black beauties were marvelous. Long legged, big of chest and shoulder, . . . they proved themselves excellent pullers. Tickle, leader of this string of Mike's, was coal black. He was a clever one, stealing anything he could get hold of, running away at the least chance, and forever cutting up. But he was a great lead dog and as game as they come. When we were in the mountains he managed to tear the muscles on one shoulder, yet despite the pain and difficulty of walking, he hobbled all the long four hundred miles back to Little America on three legs. He may have been a scamp, but no dog on the expedition was friendlier, or a better leader, or showed more uncomplaining courage and wonderful endurance.

Every man had a secret love for his own dogs, and nearly every dog showed special devotion to his driver. It was no wonder we loved them, for they showed such keen sense and often saved us serious spills in dangerous places. Probably our star actor was Dinty, leader of Norm's team. He would sit on his haunches and fan the air with his paw as though a fly was annoying him, casting his head to one side the while. And he would keep this up until we went over to pet him. If we passed down the line without talking to Dinty or petting him, he was heart-broken. Other dogs were as beautiful, as affectionate, and clever, and hard-working. But no other dog combined all these qualities. The Admiral accurately described him as a "black Malemute with soulful eyes and the disposition of Puck." . . .

On November 22, after making seventeen miles, we reached our Number Five depot. We were all quiet at supper that night. For to Norman Vaughan fell the sad duty of killing five of our dogs that had weakened. Larry had begun his supper, and then had put down his cup of cocoa with, "There is no use trying to put it off any longer. It is better to destroy those dogs than let them suffer. I'm not going to order anyone to kill them." Before any of us could say anything, Norm spoke up quickly, "See here, Larry, inasmuch as none of those dogs belong to my team, and as I have had more or less charge of the dogs, I think it is only fair for me to do this job." We all offered to relieve him of the sad task, but he stood firm. So a little white wall of snow was erected about fifty feet from the camp and it was behind this screen that the animals were shot. The rest seemed to sense what was to happen as soon as one of the doomed dogs was led away, and they would all start to whimper. At the crack of the shot, the dogs on the picket line jumped up and barked frantically. It was tragic for us all.

On the return trip to Strom camp the dogs suffered considerably from the heat. Perhaps the saddest part of this return trip was Tickle, limping along with that torn shoulder muscle of his, falling behind and catching up hours after we had made camp. He was certainly the most courageous animal I have ever seen. I remember one noon when we were through with lunch and ready to start, we could see old Tickle gamely coming into camp from a distance. We waited for him to catch up and then gave him a lift on one of the sledges. But soon we were in crevassed area again and Tickle had to get off and hobble along as best he might, for he might have been hurled into the abyss below. He seemed to understand the situation and followed along, sure that no matter when he got in, somebody would see that he had his supper. And the other dogs let him settle where he pleased. Evidently they, too, admired his pluck. The brave old fellow kept this up all the way back to Little America.

And now came trouble with Norm's team. Dinty was a great dog and a wonderful leader. But slowly he began to show signs of what might have been called temperament. He wouldn't exert himself and sulked along in the traces. He was soldiering on the job. At last, in desperation, Vaughan retired Dinty to a rear position and brought the nine months old pup, Al Smith, up into the lead. How his sensitive ears pricked forward and how his tail went up! As to Dinty, one could scarce imagine a sadder dog. The once proud waving plume of a tail was lowered, and the sparkling eyes looked duller. And so it went on, day after day, with Al proudly at the head, the shamed Dinty far in the rear.

Before we started on that last pull, when we went to harness the dogs, Vaughan gave one look at the dispirited Dinty and made a sudden change in his line-up. After all, Al Smith was just a saucy pup who would recover from any grief quickly enough. But shame Dinty by taking him back to camp in the line, and his spirit might be broken for good. He had been punished enough. So when Vaughan began bringing out his dogs, he harnessed those next to the sledge first, then the next pair, and so on. Dinty, lying with his head on his paws was secretly watching the proceedings. When all the others had been put in harness and Vaughan went back to lead Dinty out to head the line and restore him to the lead for that last pull home, the big dog was fairly trembling with excitement. Head erect and sensitive ears pointing, his eyes sparkling and that great black plume of a tail waving wildly erect, Dinty was again a lead dog to stir a driver's pride. So he brought the sledge back to camp, as he had led it out, as glorious a lead dog as ever guided his mates over snow bridges or swerved them expertly from a freshly opened crevasse which has suddenly yawned at their feet.

ALEXANDER WOOLLCOTT'S *Cocaud*

AND *the Duchess*

■ *In the heyday of radio a half-century ago, Woollcott frequently utilized dogs as a focus for his popular broadcasts. His fondness for dogs began when, as a writer on* Stars and Stripes *in France, he wrote the famous story of "Verdun Belle," a mongrel who was so devoted to a young Leatherneck that she followed him into battle at Chateau-Thierry and waited for him until he was carried out. The name of Woollcott's own poodle derives from Mme. (or Mère) Cocaud who, having lost a son in the war, catered especially to the tastes of American troops in her buvette at Savenay, a Breton village. The Duchess, a black German shepherd, was a gift of the Seeing Eye training school, a project which Woollcott vigorously supported over the years. "Cocaud," which appears in* Long, Long Ago, *a collection of Woollcott's broadcasts, is "an account of several dogs who, in their wisdom and charity, have befriended the author."*

COCAUD

On the Air

June 1939

This is Woollcott speaking—Let me admit at the start that though the words, as they fall from these old lips, are scattered at once to the four winds of radio, I think of them as addressed to a beautiful creature now listening to me in a house not fifty miles from this microphone.

Furthermore, this broadcast will be chiefly concerned with some recent goings-on under my own roof. And why not? After all, in this age there seems to be no such thing as privacy. If that's so, I see no reason why each of us should not report his own blessed events. Every man his own Winchell, that's my motto. In the spirit of that motto, I beg to announce that in the Woollcott household there is a little newcomer. It's a boy and he arrived on Thursday. He comes from good stock and it is the hope and belief of everyone in our neck of the woods that some day he will grow up to be as celebrated as his father —yes, and as charming, as intelligent and as beautiful.

Today he's extremely rattlepated and tumultuous and his hair is the hue of leaf-mould, but in another two or three months he will have taken on dignity and his coloring, they say, will be that of silvery smoke. He is, in fact, a poodle—a four-months-old French poodle. You see, I belong—and these many years have belonged—to the brother-hood of the poodle. This brotherhood is far flung and wildly miscella-neous. Among its members I can think off-hand of such actresses as Helen Hayes and Ruth Gordon, such writers as Ben Hecht and Ger-trude Stein and Booth Tarkington. Among the educators there's Presi-dent Hutchins of the University of Chicago. And the church? Why, you need look no further than His Eminence, Cardinal O'Connell of Boston. We all have one thing in common—perhaps only one. We all believe that man, as he walks this earth, can find no more engaging companion than that golden-hearted clown, the French poodle.

One and twenty years ago this October in a Y.M.C.A. canteen behind the lines during the Argonne battle I came upon a stray issue of *Collier's Weekly* and in it read Mr. Tarkington's enchanting account of his famous Gamin. Then and there I promised myself that if the war ever ended and I could dig in somewhere beyond the city pavements, I would get me such a dog and never again be without one. It took me some years, but manage it I did in time. This newcomer is the third poodle I've belonged to. Poodles there have been since about the time of Christopher Columbus. Usually they are black but sometimes they are white and sometimes the color of café-au-lait. The silver poodle is something new in the world. This one comes to me from the Blakeen Kennels at Katonah, in New York. Already in the records of the American Kennel Club—you know, the social register of the dog world—he is officially listed as Blakeen Cerulean. But I can't go around calling him that. I can't go to the door and say, "Here, Blakeen Cerulean! Here, Blakeen Cerulean!" I doubt if he'd answer. I'm sure it would do me small good to say, "Blakeen Cerulean, stop eating my bedroom slippers." So last week there was much racking of brains to find a name for him. Some were in favor of calling him Dusty and there was a time when I thought of naming him Mr. Chips. Then suddenly someone called him Cocaud and I think he'll be that till the end of the chapter.

I am no great shakes at bringing up a dog but Cocaud will be no loser by that. His education can be safely left to the Duchess. No youngster could be in better paws. For the Duchess is the sagacious and warm-hearted German shepherd dog—coal black save for a white star on her breast—who has made her home with me ever since she flunked out of The Seeing Eye. My house is on an island in a Vermont lake and the Duchess is in charge. She'll keep a friendly eye on Cocaud even though this is her busy season. In the summer her days *are* pretty much taken up with the job of ordering all speedboats off the lake. As a rule, the Duchess is benevolent in manner, but at the faint distant sound of an approaching speedboat, she becomes a fair imitation of the Hound of the Baskervilles. Her hackles rise and her eyes glow like coals in the grate. From the nearest point on the shore she bays defiance at each of these passing demons and, as it goes roaring on its way, returns to the house, smug in her conviction that she's driven it off. Thus is her ego inflated, her summer filled to the brim with a sense of worthy accomplishment. When a boat is impertinent enough to circle the island, she manages, by running at full speed, to launch her attack on it from three different points on the shore. To the boat she seems to be three hounds of the Baskervilles—enough to start the useful myth that we are protected by a pack of ferocious bloodhounds.

The Duchess is the finest dog I've ever known but I shall always remember her most fondly for the contribution she made to the gaiety of the hunting season last fall. As the first of October approached— that's when the partridge season opens in Vermont—our house became as usual the headquarters for a group of optimistic nimrods who stalk these wretched birds from dawn to dusk. Of course, in these proceedings the Duchess and I took no part. With patient politeness, we would listen while they all stood around hefting their guns in anticipation and telling hunting stories. Hunting stories! How potent they are! Better than any sleeping-pills I can buy at a drug store.

Dull and early on the morning of October first, the first boat of the season started for the mainland laden to the gunnels with sportsmen, a small arsenal and a pack of yipping bird-dogs. The Duchess and I didn't even get up to see them off and we were dozing in front of the fire when they returned at sundown—muddy, weary and more than a little crestfallen. Apparently they hadn't seen—certainly they hadn't molested—a single partridge. And they drew this blank not only on the first day but on the second, the third, and the fourth. Even so, they professed to be having a grand time and didn't seem ruffled until I began praising them for their unfailing kindness to our feathered friends. Indeed, they didn't get really sore until I named them the Audubon Society.

On the next morning, their luck turned to the extent of about one partridge a day. These trophies were hung on the outside of the house high under the roof. It was decided that when there were four they would make a good dinner. Apparently the Duchess thought so too, for just before the cook went out to pluck them, the Duchess took a running jump, went up the side of the house and collected the lot. As the cook came out of the kitchen door, the Duchess, bless her heart, was just polishing off the last one. In my part of Vermont they still speak of her as Woollcott's bird-dog.

Well, to such an experienced and resourceful teacher I will gladly entrust the education of Cocaud. It's my hope that when business takes me up and down the country, he will be able to go along. That will, I think, be all right with him. Ever since some pre-historic Fido decided to cast in his lot with the strange new biped called *homo sapiens*, it has always been a dog's idea of happiness to be with the man that belongs to him. This is true even when the old fool is silly enough to live in a trap of steel and concrete like any great city. New York, for instance. There's a ridiculous habitation no more fit for a dog than it is for a man. There's hardly a stretch of dirt there you can call your own.

In this connection let me tell you about a night in Boston. When Symphony Hall was crowded to the doors with a meeting in behalf of The Seeing Eye—that unique school where the German shepherds are trained as guide-dogs for the blind. One of these had just gone through her paces on the platform and Jack Humphrey, the trainer, was answering questions. These Seeing Eye dogs are workers just as you and I are workers and their job is no cinch. Sometimes this afflicts the sentimental and one woman in the back of the hall asked, "Don't the poor dogs ever have any fun?" As if he were a little embarrassed, Jack paused for a moment and then said, "Well, ma'am, it depends on what you mean by fun." And then quickly he put some questions to the audience. They all of them loved dogs, didn't they? And many of them owned dogs, too, didn't they? How many? A very forest of hands went up in the air. "Well," said Jack, "where are your dogs now?" For a moment Symphony Hall was filled with a kind of guilty silence. Each person present, in order to be there at all, had had to chain his dog in the cellar at home or lock it up in the bathroom. A blind man's dog is with him every hour of the twenty-four and asks no greater happiness on earth.

Maybe Cocaud will feel that way. Already he's beginning to manifest a puzzling enthusiasm for me. As for my bedroom slippers, he's nuts about them. I wonder if those two playwrights who say they're writing a comedy for me this fall could be induced to work in a scene for Cocaud. All poodles are comedians and it ought not be difficult for Cocaud to master a simple role. Something like the one written years ago for Lizzie, the Fishhound. Lizzie used to play in vaudeville with Harry Kelly. It was the whole point of Lizzie's part that she should ignore every command Kelly gave her. Harry would thunder at her, "Lie down!" and she wouldn't move. "Good dog." She was, he said, a mighty valuable dog. I can hear him now across the years. "Mighty valuable dog. Mighty valuable dog. Wuth a quarter."

Speaking of valuable dogs, I remember how baffled The Seeing Eye people were by one of their first graduates. He was a piano-tuner and an inspector from the school, visiting in his city, arranged to find out how he and his dog were making out. The appointment was for the next morning at eleven and although the rain was pouring in torrents the blind man arrived on the dot. But his escort was an old woman. Where was his dog? "What, bring my fine dog out on a day like this! Why she might catch her death of cold." So, instead, he had brought his grandmother.

All of which—as I said at the beginning of this broadcast—is meant for the ears of a beautiful creature now listening to me (with what interest, of course, I cannot tell) in a house not fifty miles away. That house is in Katonah, New York, where Cocaud himself was born. Just as all boys in any school glow with vicarious pride over the achievement of any of their number—just as every boy at Illinois, for example, used to bask in the glory of Red Grange—so I've no doubt that Cocaud is even now swanking around the island telling tall tales to the Duchess about the gleaming white poodle at the kennels where he used to live. Yes, ma'am, an international champion and sweeping all before him. This marvel's name is Eiger. I wonder if Eiger likes hearing his name come out of that noise-box in the library. Eiger. Eiger. Here's talking at you.

E. B. WHITE'S *Boston Terrier*
AND *Fred*

■ *Apparently underlying E. B. White's numerous portraits of dogs in his letters and essays is the assumption enunciated in "A Boston Terrier": "A dog more than any other creature . . . gets interested in one subject, theme, or object, in life and pursues it with a fixity of purpose which would be inspiring to Man if it weren't so troublesome." In the first essay, the terrier's idée fixe is a pet rock, the "Stone Supreme," which he guards and gnaws with disastrous devotion. In the second essay, the dachshund Fred's fixation is a broader determination to reorder the world to his own design. White's dogs tend to be heavily anthropomorphic—mirrors of ourselves or implicit caricatures of human types or acquaintances. Yet however ridiculous or troublesome White may have found the canine breed, he clearly also found it indispensable to a satisfying existence in his Maine retreat, inhabited as it was by Fred, Jones, Maggie, Mac, Moses, Raffles, and, no doubt, many others.*

A BOSTON TERRIER

I would like to hand down a dissenting opinion in the case of the Camel ad which shows a Boston terrier relaxing. I can string along with cigarette manufacturers to a certain degree, but when it comes to the temperament and habits of terriers, I shall stand my ground.

The ad says: "A dog's nervous system resembles our own." I don't think a dog's nervous system resembles my own in the least. A dog's nervous system is in a class by itself. If it resembles anything at all, it resembles the New York Edison Company's power plant. This is particularly true of Boston terriers, and if the Camel people don't know that, they have never been around dogs.

The ad says: "But when a dog's nerves tire, he obeys his instincts —he relaxes." This, I admit, is true. But I should like to call attention to the fact that it sometimes takes days, even weeks, before a dog's nerves tire. In the case of terriers it can run into months.

I knew a Boston terrier once (he is now dead and, so far as I know, relaxed) whose nerves stayed keyed up from the twenty-fifth of one June to the sixth of the following July, without one minute's peace for anybody in the family. He was an old dog and he was blind in one eye, but his infirmities caused no diminution in his nervous power. During the period of which I speak, the famous period of his greatest excitation, he not only raised a type of general hell which startled even his closest friends and observers, but he gave a mighty clever excuse. He said it was love.

"I'm in love," he would scream. (He could scream just like a hurt child.) "I'm in love and I'm going *crazy.*"

Day and night it was all the same. I tried everything to soothe him. I tried darkness, cold water dashed in the face, the lash, long quiet talks, warm milk administered internally, threats, promises, and close confinement in remote locations. At last, after about a week of it, I went down the road and had a chat with the lady who owned the object of our terrier's affection. It was she who finally cleared up the situation.

"Oh," she said, wearily, "if it's that bad, let him out."

I hadn't thought of anything as simple as that myself, but I am a creature of infinite reserve. As a matter of record, it turned out to be not so simple—the terrier got run over by a motor car one night while returning from his amorous adventures, suffering a complete paralysis of the hip but no assuagement of the nervous system; and the little Scotty bitch returned to Washington, D. C., and a Caesarian.

I am not through with the Camel people yet. Love is not the only thing that can keep a dog's nerves in a state of perpetual jangle. A dog, more than any other creature, it seems to me, gets interested in one subject, theme, or object, in life, and pursues it with a fixity of purpose which would be inspiring to Man if it weren't so troublesome. One dog gets absorbed in one thing, another dog in another. When I was a boy there was a smooth-haired fox terrier (in those days nobody ever heard of a fox terrier that *wasn't* smooth-haired) who became interested, rather late in life, in a certain stone. The stone was about the size of an egg. As far as I could see, it was like a million other stones—but to him it was the Stone Supreme.

He kept it with him day and night, slept with it, ate with it, played with it, analyzed it, took it on little trips (you would often see him three blocks from home, trotting along on some shady errand, his stone safe in his jaws). He used to lie by the hour on the porch of his house, chewing the stone with an expression half tender, half petulant. When he slept he merely enjoyed a muscular suspension: his nerves were still up and around, adjusting the bed clothes, tossing and turning.

He permitted people to throw the stone for him and people would. But if the stone lodged somewhere he couldn't get to he raised such an uproar that it was absolutely necessary that the stone be returned, for the public peace. His absorption was so great it brought wrinkles to his face, and he grew old before his time. I think he used to worry that somebody was going to pitch the stone into a lake or a bog, where it would be irretrievable. He wore off every tooth in his jaw, wore them right down to the gums, and they became mere brown vestigial bumps. His breath was awful (he panted night and day) and his eyes were alight with an unearthly zeal. He died in a fight with another dog. I have always suspected it was because he tried to hold the stone in his mouth all through the battle. The Camel people will just have to take my word for it: that dog was a living denial of the whole theory of relaxation. He was a paragon of nervous tension, from the moment he first laid eyes on his slimy little stone till the hour of his death.

The advertisement speaks of the way humans "prod" themselves to endeavor—so that they keep on and on working long after they should quit. The inference is that a dog never does that. But I have a dog right now that can prod himself harder and drive himself longer than any human I ever saw. This animal is a dachshund, and I shall spare you the long dull inanities of his innumerable obsessions. His particular study (or mania) at the moment is a black-and-white kitten that my wife gave me for Christmas thinking that what my life needed was something else that could move quickly from one place in the room to another. The dachshund began his research on Christmas eve when the kitten arrived "secretly" in the cellar, and now, five months later, is taking his Ph.D. still working late at night on it, every night. If he could write a book about that cat, it would make *Middletown* look like the work of a backward child.

I'll be glad to have the Camel people study this animal in one of his relaxed moods, but they will have to bring their own seismograph. Even curled up cozily in a chair, dreaming of his cat, he quivers like an aspen.

From BEDFELLOWS

I am lying here in my private sick bay on the east side of town between Second and Third avenues, watching starlings from the vantage point of bed. Three Democrats are in bed with me: Harry Truman (in a stale copy of the *Times*), Adlai Stevenson (in *Harper's*), and Dean Acheson (in a book called *A Democrat Looks at His Party*). I take Democrats to bed with me for lack of a dachshund, although as a matter of fact on occasions like this I am almost certain to be visited by the ghost of Fred, my dash-hound everlasting, dead these many years. In life, Fred always attended the sick, climbing right into bed with the patient like some lecherous old physician, and making a bad situation worse. All this dark morning I have reluctantly entertained him upon the rumpled blanket, felt his oppressive weight, and heard his fraudulent report. He was an uncomfortable bedmate when alive; death has worked little improvement—I still feel crowded, still wonder why I put up with his natural rudeness and his pretensions.

The only thing I used to find agreeable about him in bed was his smell, which for some reason was nonirritating to my nose and evocative to my mind, somewhat in the way that a sudden whiff of the cow barn or of bone meal on a lawn in springtime carries sensations of the richness of earth and of experience. Fred's aroma has not deserted him; it wafts over me now, as though I had just removed the stopper from a vial of cheap perfume. His aroma has not deserted the last collar he wore, either. I ran across this great, studded strap not long ago when I was rummaging in a cabinet. I raised it cautiously toward my nose, fearing a quill stab from his last porcupine. The collar was extremely high—had lost hardly 10 percent of its potency.

Fred was sold to me for a dachshund, but I was in a buying mood and would have bought the puppy if the storekeeper had said he was an Irish Wolfschmidt. He was only a few weeks old when I closed the deal, and he was in real trouble. In no time at all, his troubles cleared up and mine began. Thirteen years later he died, and by rights *my* troubles should have cleared up. But I can't say they have. Here I am, seven years after his death, still sharing a fever bed with him and, what is infinitely more burdensome, still feeling the compulsion to write about him. I sometimes suspect that subconsciously I'm trying to revenge myself by turning him to account, and thus recompensing myself for the time and money he cost me.

He was red and low-posted and long-bodied like a dachshund, and when you glanced casually at him he certainly gave the quick impression of being a dachshund. But if you went at him with a tape measure, and forced him onto scales, the dachshund theory collapsed. The papers that came with him were produced hurriedly and in an illicit atmosphere in a back room of the pet shop, and are most unconvincing. However, I have no reason to unsettle the Kennel Club; the fraud, if indeed it was a fraud, was ended in 1948, at the time of his death. So much of his life was given to shady practices, it is only fitting that his pedigree should have been (as I believe it was) a forgery.

I have been languishing here, looking out at the lovely branches of the plane tree in the sky above our city back yard. Only starlings and house sparrows are in view at this season, but soon other birds will show up. . . . Fred was a window gazer and bird watcher, particularly during his later years, when hardened arteries slowed him up and made it necessary for him to substitute sedentary pleasures for active sport. I think of him as he used to look on our bed in Maine—an old four-poster, too high from the floor for him to reach unassisted. Whenever the bed was occupied during the daylight hours, whether because one of us was sick or was napping, Fred would appear in the doorway and enter without knocking. On his big gray face would be a look of quiet amusement (at having caught somebody in bed during the daytime) coupled with his usual look of fake respectability. Whoever occupied the bed would reach down, seize him by the loose folds of his thick neck, and haul him painfully up. He dreaded this maneuver, and so did the occupant of the bed. There was far too much dead weight involved for anybody's comfort. But Fred was always willing to put up with being hoisted in order to gain the happy heights, as, indeed, he was willing to put up with far greater discomforts—such as a mouthful of porcupine quills—when there was some prize at the end.

Once up, he settled into his pose of bird watching propped luxuriously against a pillow, as close as he could get to the window, his great soft brown eyes alight with expectation and scientific knowledge. He seemed never to tire of his work. He watched steadily and managed to give the impression that he was a secret agent of the Department of Justice. Spotting a flicker or a starling on the wing, he would turn and make a quick report.

"I just saw an eagle go by," he would say. "It was carrying a baby."

This was not precisely a lie. Fred was like a child in many ways, and sought always to blow things up to proportions that satisfied his imagination and his love of adventure. He was the Cecil B. deMille of dogs. He was a zealot, and I have just been reminded of him by a quote from one of the Democrats sharing my bed—Acheson quoting Brandeis. "The greatest dangers to liberty," said Mr. Brandeis, "lurk in insidious encroachment by men of zeal, well-meaning but without understanding." Fred saw in every bird, every squirrel, every housefly, every rat, every skunk, every porcupine, a security risk and a present danger to his republic. He had a dossier on almost every living creature, as well as on several inanimate objects, including my son's football.

Although birds fascinated him, his real hope as he watched the big shade trees outside the window was that a red squirrel would show up. When he sighted a squirrel, Fred would straighten up from his pillow, tense his frame, and then, in a moment or two, begin to tremble. The knuckles of his big forelegs, unstable from old age, would seem to go into spasm, and he would sit there with his eyes glued on the squirrel and his front legs alternately collapsing under him and bearing his weight again.

I find it difficult to convey the peculiar character of this ignoble old vigilante, my late and sometimes lamented companion. What was there about him so different from the many other dogs I've owned that he keeps recurring and does not, in fact, seem really dead at all? My wife used to claim that Fred was deeply devoted to me, and in a certain sense he was, but his was the devotion of an opportunist. He knew that on the farm I took the overall view and traveled pluckily from one trouble spot to the next. He dearly loved this type of work. It was not his habit to tag along faithfully behind me, as a collie might, giving moral support and sometimes real support. He ran a troubleshooting business of his own and was usually at the scene ahead of me, compounding the trouble and shooting in the air. The word "faithful" is an adjective I simply never thought of in connection with Fred. He differed from most dogs in that he tended to knock down, rather than build up, the master's ego. Once he had outgrown the capers of puppyhood, he never again caressed me or anybody else during his life. The only time he was ever discovered in an attitude that suggested affection was when I was in the driver's seat of our car and he would lay his heavy head on my right knee. This, I soon perceived, was not affection, it was nausea. Drooling always followed, and the whole thing was extremely inconvenient, because the weight of his head made me press too hard on the accelerator.

Fred devoted his life to deflating me and succeeded admirably. His attachment to our establishment, though untinged with affection, was strong nevertheless, and vibrant. It was simply that he found in our persons, in our activities, the sort of complex, disorderly society that fired his imagination and satisfied his need for tumult and his quest for truth. After he had subdued six or seven porcupines, we realized that his private war against porcupines was an expensive bore, so we took to tying him, making him fast to any tree or wheel or post or log that was at hand, to keep him from sneaking off into the woods. I think of him as always at the end of some outsize piece of rope. Fred's disgust at these confinements was great, but he improved his time, nonetheless, in a thousand small diversions. He never just lay and rested. Within the range of his tether, he continued to explore, dissect, botanize, conduct post-mortems, excavate, experiment, expropriate, savor, masticate, regurgitate. He had no contemplative life, but he held as a steady gleam the belief that under the commonplace stone and behind the unlikely piece of driftwood lay the stuff of high adventure and the opportunity to save the nation. . . .

Fred was an unbeliever. He worshiped no personal God, no Supreme Being. He certainly did not worship *me*. . . . I respected this quirk in Fred, this inability to conform to conventional canine standards of religious feeling. And in the miniature democracy that was, and is, our household he lived undisturbed and at peace with his conscience. . . .

Anyway, it's pleasant here in bed with all these friendly Democrats and Republicans, every one of them a dedicated man, with all these magazine and newspaper clippings, with Fred, watching the starlings against the wintry sky, and the prospect of another presidential year, with all its passions and its distortions and its dissents and its excesses and special interests. Fred died from a life of excesses, and I don't mind if I do, too. . . . It makes me eager to rise and meet the new day, as Fred used to rise to his with the complete conviction that through vigilance and good works all porcupines, all cats, all skunks, all squirrels, all houseflies, all footballs, all evil birds in the sky could be successfully brought to account and the scene made safe and pleasant for the sensible individual—namely, him. However distorted was his crazy vision of the beautiful world, however perverse his scheme for establishing an order of goodness by murdering every creature that seemed to him bad, I had to hand him this: he really worked at it. . . .

One day last fall I wandered down through the orchard and into the woods to pay a call at Fred's grave. The trees were bare; wild apples hung shamelessly from the grapevine that long ago took over the tree. The old dump, which is no longer used and which goes out of sight during the leafy months, lay exposed and candid—rusted pots and tin cans and sundries. The briers had lost some of their effectiveness, the air was good, and the little dingle, usually so mean and inconsiderable, seemed to have acquired stature. Fred's headstone, ordinarily in collapse, was bolt upright, and I wondered whether he had quieted down at last. I felt uneasy suddenly, as the quick do sometimes feel when in the presence of the dead, and my uneasiness went to my bladder. Instead of laying a wreath, I watered an alder and came away.

This grave is the only grave I visit with any regularity—in fact, it is the only grave I visit at all. I have relatives lying in cemeteries here and there around the country, but I do not feel any urge to return to them, and it strikes me as odd that I should return to the place where an old dog lies in a shabby bit of woodland next to a private dump. Besides being an easy trip (one for which I need make no preparation) it is a natural journey—I really go down there to see what's doing. (Fred himself used to scout the place every day when he was alive.) I do not experience grief when I am down there, nor do I pay tribute to the dead. I feel a sort of overall sadness that has nothing to do with the grave or its occupant. Often I feel extremely well in that rough cemetery, and sometimes flush a partridge. But I feel sadness at All Last Things, too, which is probably a purely selfish, or turned-in, emotion —sorrow not at my dog's death but at my own, which hasn't even occurred yet but which saddens me just to think about in such pleasant surroundings.

ERIC KNIGHT'S *Lassie*

■ *Undoubtedly the best-known dog among Americans of all ages during the past generation has been Lassie, who, owing to a long series of films, is viewed as an exemplary good Samaritan. The original Lassie, however, was an inhabitant of Yorkshire whose distinguishing trait was her homing instinct which insistently drew her to be with her young and devoted master. Her chronicler-creator, Eric Knight, was a Yorkshireman who as a young man came to Canada and later to the United States. A versatile journalist and novelist and Anglo-American patriot, he was involved in both World Wars. In the second he was a major in the American army and on a special mission in 1943 he died in a plane crash in Surinam. Prior to writing* Lassie Come-Home, *he had hearkened back to his English past in his humorous* The Flying Yorkshireman; *and, after* Lassie, *in his widely read* This Above All *(1941) he dealt with the impact of the second World War on the thoughtful youth of England.*

From LASSIE COME-HOME

Everyone in Greenall Bridge knew Sam Carraclough's Lassie. Greenall Bridge is in the county of Yorkshire, and of all places in the world it is here that the dog is really king. Its men all agreed that if a finer dog than Sam Carraclough's tricolor collie had ever been bred in Greenall Bridge, it must have been long before they were born.

One day Sam's boy, Joe, had come home bubbling with excitement.

"Mother! I come out of school today, and who do you think was sitting there waiting for me? Lassie!" Lassie was waiting at the school gate the next day, and the next. For four years it had always been the same.

For three years the Duke [of Rudling] had been trying to buy Lassie from Sam, and Sam had merely stood his ground. Yet sometimes there comes a time in a man's life when he must eat his pride so that his family may eat bread.

The dog was not there! That was all Joe Carraclough knew. Perhaps someone had stolen Lassie! He ran home to tell his mother. "Mother? Mother—something's happened to Lassie!" Joe knew that there was something wrong. "Ye might as well know it right off, Joe," she said. "Lassie won't be waiting at school for ye no more. Because she's sold."

The boy rose and stood by his mother. "Look Joe, ye know things aren't going so well for us these days and—well, we couldn't afford to keep her, that's all." . . .

Priscilla [the Duke's twelve-year-old granddaughter] saw, lying there, a great black-white-and-golden-sable collie. She lay there, her eyes not turning toward the people who stood looking at her. Priscilla bent down and called quickly: "Come, collie!" For just one second the great brown eyes of the collie turned to the girl, deep brown eyes that seemed full of brooding and sadness.

When Joe came out of school, he could not believe his eyes. He ran to his dog, and in his moment of wild joy he knelt beside her. Lassie had escaped! Mrs. Carraclough warmed a pan of food, and she and her son stood watching Lassie eat happily. But the man [Sam] never once turned his eyes toward the dog that had been his. There was the sound of footsteps and Hynes [the Duke's kennel man] came in, walked quickly to the collie and slipped the noose over her head. [After repeated later escapes Lassie was always returned to the Duke by Joe and his father, who told Joe:] "Tha might as well put Lassie clean out o' mind, because tha's never to see her no more. She's run away her last time; he's taken her up to his place in Scotland."

"Father. Is it very far to Scotland?"

"A long, long way, Joe. Much farther than tha'll ever travel."

. . .

Had it been any other part of the day [it was nearly four o'clock], Lassie might have returned to Hynes as he bid her. It had been on one of the newly ordered walks, with Lassie going along obediently, that he wanted to show Lassie "who was boss." And so, quite needlessly, he suddenly tugged on the leash. The leash slipped over Lassie's head.

She was free! It was time to go for the boy! She wheeled and began trotting away. There was nothing to tell her that the rendezvous she would keep was hundreds of miles away. She broke from her trot into a gentle lope.

Priscilla and her grandfather rode up the road and halted by the iron gate to the estate. "I'll open it," the girl said and swung it slowly back on its hinges. Hynes was shouting: "Close that gate, Miss Priscilla!" For a second she swung her weight back on it. But then she saw again a certain picture in her mind—of a village boy standing beside the meshed wire of a run, saying to his dog: "Bide here forever—and don't never come home no more." Priscilla began swinging the gate wide open. "Good-bye, Lassie," she said, softly. "Good-bye and—good luck!"

But now Lassie had learned one thing. She must keep away from men. That first night Lassie traveled steadily. Whenever a path ran to the south, she followed it. For the first four days Lassie traveled without pause, resting only during the nights. On the fifth day a new demand began to gnaw at her senses. It was the call of hunger. Suddenly, on the path she saw what her nose had warned her of—a weasel and by his side the freshly killed body of a rabbit. She came near, and picked up the game. She smelled it again. It smelled good. It was food.

So the dog went, day after day. She could not know that the instinctive straight line toward home would bring her to an impasse against the great lochs of Scotland. Yet at the shore of the great loch, Lassie did not surrender her purpose. Day after day she worked west. A week [later] the long loch stretched as a barrier that a dog could not understand.

She was moving more slowly now, for the pads of her feet were bruised and sore, and between those pads on the right forefoot a thorn was festering. The loch had narrowed to a river. Lassie looked at the white, tumbling water. Then, boldly springing, she launched her body far out into the water. Again and again the current tumbled her with crushing force. The current drew her down, and she disappeared. Then fighting, swimming, driving, she made the landing. At last she was free—free to go south.

It was long past nightfall when she denned up where a clump of gorse arched over beside a field-wall. In the tumbling river she had broken one rib and bruised badly her hind leg. She could travel no farther. For six days she lay, almost without a move. From the festering sore the thorn had worked its way. Lassie cleaned the wound. Her bad hind leg hung, not touching the ground. Hobbling across the field, she found the streamlet and lapped—the first time she had drunk for a week. For two more days she rested there. But of food, she had none. Then, stiffly, she crossed the stream. Going slowly, she struck out to the south.

By the great Scottish industrial city the river is broad—and there are aged bridges that have carried traffic north and south for centuries. Over one of those busy bridges Lassie trotted. She went along the pavement to the south. She did not heed the truck pulling up beside her. Something was moving through the air. About her was a net that strangled her efforts. For a full minute she fought, slashing at the imprisoning web. But she was only held the tighter. A thong was being twisted about her muzzle. Another thong went about her neck, another was binding her legs together. She felt the net being lifted; then she was being beaten over the head. And then the men halted their beating, for a voice came, very clear, from the crowd: "Here, you don't have to treat that dog as savagely as that!"

"Very sorry, mum; but it's my duty. There's a lot of mad dogs around—and a dog catcher's got to do his duty."

The van drew into a courtyard [and] backed up tight against a raised entrance. Other dogs in the van had lifted their voices in clamor. But Lassie had lain still, like a captive queen among lesser prisoners. The man entered the van with a small leash. Down they came over the tailboard of the van, and he leaned down to unslip the leash. In that flash, Lassie was free. Down the corridor she went. Hands grabbed at her as she raced along. There were many doors, all closed. And then escape came. For one of the forbidding doors opened, and a voice sounded: "What's going on out here? Do you realize there's a Court of Law sitting . . ." That was as far as he got. For at that moment a tawny figure streaked by him. Then he shut the door. At last, in a corner, Lassie stood at bay. Bearing the net, the two men entered the court. "We'll soon ha' her out o' here, Your Lordship," one said. But as he spoke, Lassie wheeled away. Above her was an open window. She leaped to the ledge—and then stood there in hesitation. There was a sheer drop of twenty feet to concrete below. On the ledge Lassie trembled. Off to the left was the roof of the van only ten feet below. Then she leaped. Out she drove, as far as she could, toward the top of the van. Reaching out with her forelegs, she just touched. Then she dropped to the ground heavily; and she lay, stunned. The two men made their way to the courtyard. They looked about in amazement.

She was not there. "Donnell, where is she?" "Gone over the wall, Mr. Fairgusson!" "Six foot—and she should be dead, Donnell."

Slowly, steadily, Lassie came across a field. She was going at a painful walk, still continuing to go south. The track became mud, then a puddle, and the puddle was the edge of a river. Lassie, wading forward tentatively, went deeper and deeper. She began swimming. And when at last she reached the other shore, she was almost too weak to climb the bank. There, at last, she dropped. But she was in England! Lassie lay on one side. Her eyes were glazed. Darkness came with its night sounds. Dawn came. Lassie rose slowly. She set out—going south.

Together they [Daniel and Dolly Fadden] hurried out into the night, leaning against the gusts of wind and rain. There she saw what her husband had found—a dog, lying in the ditch. "It's too done up to walk," he shouted. The two old people brought Lassie into the warmth of the hearth and laid her on the rug. "I doubt it'll live till the morn," the man said. Awkwardly the old man bent, rubbing the dog's drenched coat. Only dimly Lassie knew of the saucer of warm milk set beside her head. Then she felt her head being lifted. She gulped, once—twice—three times. Firmly the old woman planted herself in the rocking chair for a night of watching. A week later Mrs. Fadden looked over her glasses and beamed at Lassie, lying on the rug, her ears erect. Her beautiful dog, *her* dog! "Oh, if anyone owns it! Find out, will ye, Dan? Go ask around." It was a long afternoon. At last she heard footsteps. "I asked all around the place—everywhere—and nobody seems to ha' lost her." "Then she's ours!"

Lassie lay on the rug. Strength had returned in the three weeks in her new home. The one driving force of her life was wakened. As the clock moved round toward four, it became maddening. Lassie went to the door. She whined and lifted her head. Then she began pacing back and forth. The woman shook her head. "I didn't tell ye, but the last three days, Dan, she's not eating. She's not happy. Dan, she's going somewhere. She's on her way." The next afternoon when the time neared four o'clock, and Lassie rose, their eyes followed her. And when Lassie whined at the door, they both sighed. The woman opened the door. Side by side, the old man and his wife followed Lassie out to the road. There for a moment the dog stood. For a second, the old woman wished to call the dog back. But she lifted her head. "It's all right, then, dog. If ye must go—awa' wi' ye." Lassie caught the word "go." She turned, looked back once as in farewell, and then started across the field. She was going south again. They went into the cottage and sat at the table. But neither of them ate.

Lassie plodded on. Now she was crossing a great, high moor, where the wind swept without halt. The snowstorm drove from behind her. She found it hard to keep going. At last she staggered and fell. The snow was too deep. She began plunging at it like a horse, but before very long she found herself utterly exhausted. She gave a long cry—the cry of a dog lost, cold and helpless. Lassie sank to the ground. Below that white blanket she lay, exhausted but warm.

It was a long way from Greenall Bridge to the Duke of Rudling's place in Scotland. For an animal it would be a thousand miles through strange terrain with nothing but instinct to tell direction. Yet, in his heart Joe Carraclough tried to believe that somehow his dog would be there someday, waiting by the school gate.

Always, when school ended, Joe tried to prepare himself not to be disappointed, because there could be no dog there. And so coming across the schoolyard that day, Joe could not believe his eyes. There, walking the last few yards to the gate was—his dog! He stood, for the coming of the dog was terrible—a crawl rather than a walk. He raced across the yard and fell to his knees. This was a dog that lay, weakly trying to lift a head that would no longer lift. "I must get her home quick!" the boy was saying. Ian Cawper stepped forward. His great arms cradled the dog. Joe raced along the street and burst into the cottage: "Mother! Father! Lassie's come home!" Not a word did his parents speak to him. Instead, they both worked over the dog. Joe watched how his father spooned in the warm liquid, he saw how it drooled out again. He saw his mother warm up a blanket and wrap it round the dog. "Pneumonia," his father said at last. "She's not strong enough now . . ." It was his mother who seemed to be alive and strong. "I just *won't* be beat," she said. She took down a vase. The copper pennies came into her hand. His father hurried out into the night. When he came back he was carrying bundles—eggs and a small bottle of brandy—precious and costly things in that home. In the morning his mother was still on the rug, and the fire was still burning warm. The dog, swathed in blankets, lay quiet. That was one day. There was another when Joe's mother sighed with pleasure, for as she prepared the milk, the dog stirred. When the bowl was set down, she put down her head and lapped. . . .

The Duke of Rudling got out of a car. "Go away," the boy said fiercely. "Thy tyke's not here. It's not Lassie." Then they all heard the voice of Sam Carraclough: "Does it look like any dog that belongs to thee?" He saw his father standing with a dog the like of which few men had ever seen before. He understood. He knew that if a dog coper could treat a dog so its bad points came to look like good ones, he could also make its good ones look like bad ones. But the Duke knew many things too. Slowly he knelt down and picked up a forepaw. And those eyes stared steadily at the underside of the paw, seeing only the five black pads, crossed and recrossed with half-healed scars. "Sam Carraclough," he said. "This is no dog of mine. Not for a single second did she ever belong to me! Four hundred miles! I wouldn't ha' believed it." He turned. "You working? I need somebody at my kennels. And I think you must know—a lot—about dogs. So there. That's settled." It was afterward that the girl [Priscilla] said, "Grandfather, you are kind about the dog." "Nonsense," he growled. "For five years I've sworn I'd have that dog. And now I've got her."

Each weekday Joe would come out of school and greet his dog. Yet, there came a time when Lassie appeared no more at the school gate. However, Joe didn't seem to care. As he went along the gravel path of the Duke's grounds, he saw the girl again. "How is Lassie?" Joe smiled. "You can come and see." He led the way to the scullery, where a great, low box was set. And in the box was Lassie, and piled about her were seven plump, sleeping balls of fur. "You see, we keep her here because she's a home dog, Lassie is. Ye're a come-home dog, aren't ye, Lassie? Ye're my Lassie Come-home."

GERTRUDE STEIN'S *Baskets*

■ *Just how much time the two poodles of Gertrude Stein spent at her famous Parisian salon at 27 rue de Fleurus is not clear, for she usually speaks of them as being in the company of children or villagers. Stein writes of walking with Basket I in the mountain village of Culoz. As a "war dog," Basket II must have returned to the same village in the occupied zone of eastern France with Stein and her secretary-companion Alice B. Toklas, for the children and the villagers continually compare the two poodles. The character of the second Basket, however, emerges more distinctly through Stein's description of his behavior on trains, his reactions to German soldiers, and his nervousness at the celebration of the American liberation of France. Through her pride in and devotion to her two Baskets she emerges as the pragmatic, self-reliant, whimsical, patriotic, middle-class American that she considered herself to be.*

From PARIS FRANCE

Our dog's name is Basket and the French like that, it sounds so well in French and goes well with Monsieur, the children all call him Monsieur Basket. That was our first Basket. We did love the first Basket and he was shaved like a real poodle and he did fait le beau and he could say how do you do and he was ten years old and last autumn just after our return to Paris he died. We did cry and cry and finally every one said get another dog and get it right away. Henry Daniel-Rops said get another as like Basket as possible call him by the same name and gradually there will be confusion and you will not know which Basket it is.

And then I saw Picasso, and he said no, never get the same kind of dog. I tried it once and it was awful, the new one reminded me of the old one and the more he looked like him the worse it was. No never get the same kind of dog, get an Afghan hound, he has one, and Jean Hugo had said I could have one, but they are so sad, I said, that's all right for a Spaniard, but I don't like dogs to be sad, and as I went out he repeated not the same no not the same. So we tried to have the same and not to have the same and then at last we found another Basket and he is very gay and I cannot say that the confusion between the old and new has yet taken place.

I was a little worried what Picasso would say when he saw the new Basket who was so like the old Basket but fortunately the new Basket does stand on his legs in some indefinable way a little the way an Afghan hound stands on his although the new Basket is pure poodle, and I pointed this out to Picasso when we and our dogs met on the street and that did rather reconcile him to it. And now this Basket being a war-dog, that is living in war-time is very much a village dog and although the village spends a great deal of time discussing whether he is more or less beautiful than the last one, whether he is bigger and whether he is more affectionate the children like him but they treat him with less respect, they call him Basket familiarly they do not call him Monsieur Basket, there is that difference in their character. But for all that he is a very sweet Basket, any dog one loves is a very sweet dog.

From WARS I HAVE SEEN

Basket I. Just to-night June 1943 I was out walking in the twilight in the mountain village of Culoz and my dog Basket was running around and a young man in working clothes said he is a nice dog but I have been whistling to him and he wont come. Oh I said, you have to do more than whistle, you have to talk English.

To-day we were at Aix-les-Bains at the station. [A]ll trains go very slowly now, and all the French people were as if they were at a theatre that was not interesting and then our train came in and I got on it with my white dog Basket and the French people were pleased, Basket was the real circus, he was a theatre they found interesting.

I like a thing they [the French] say if they say it every time they feel it. They say it of my dog Basket, every time they see him and they see him any time and they always say look at him you would take him for a sheep. And so all this time everybody speaks of the Germans, and nobody says anything except that the Germans are pretty sick now [September 1943].

Basket II. It is interesting. We have Basket II. He is a pedigreed dog, twenty generations are behind him and all of them German. The other Basket was unpedigreed and entirely French. And we have a cat, the peasants who gave it to us called it Hitler because of his mustache and Basket had not been friendly with him but no matter. But now suddenly he chases him away. Is it an omen.

And we got off dog and all because of course Basket is always with us he likes train trips he did not at first but he does now because they admire him and they feed him, French people even in these days of no bread and no sugar cannot see a dog without offering him some bread and some sugar if they are eating and in these days anybody in the train is eating.

They are still here the Germans and Basket our dog has gone out for the evening it worries us but we expect he will come back again. Although you never can tell with soldiers, they like dogs and he is a very pretty one. And nobody knows why they are here nor how long they will stay.

The mayor finally persuaded the Germans that there were no mountain boys in the mountain back of us. They left. And the telephone goes again, and I can let the dog out again the dog Basket and we can go walking again in February nineteen forty-four.

A little later two little baby goats followed my dog Basket and there was great trouble in sending them back because their mother having died they had been mothered by a sheep, and they took Basket for a sheep and their mother. Basket was not flattered, he was very annoyed.

I came home having put my dog on the leash and when I got home there were about a hundred of these Germans in the garden in the house all over the place, poor Basket was so horrified that he could not even bark, I took him up to my bedroom and he just sat and shivered. They left the next morning and Basket has hardly barked since and I heard to-day that they shot a dog in the village because they said he barked, perhaps Basket will never bark again, I am trying to induce him to bark again, it is not right that a dog should be silent.

Paris was taken at noon and they say that Americans are at Aix-les-Bains only twenty-five kilometers away how we want to see them. I naturally wanted my dog Basket to participate and so I took him down to the local barber and I said wont you shave him and make him elegant, it is not right when the Americans come along that the only French poodle in Culoz and owned by Americans should not be elegant, so perspiring freely all of us including Basket, he had his paws shaved and his muzzle shaved and he was elegant and took part in the evening's celebration all the little children, said Basket Basket come here Basket, they do say it beautifully and then there was a blare of trumpets and naturally he was frightened and tried to run away, so I tied him with a handkerchief and the effort was not so elegant but we were all proud of ourselves just the same.

Scotty

AND *Rex*

■ *The title of one of Thurber's books,* Men, Women, and Dogs, *suggests the range of characters whom he depicts as beset by bizarre frustrations. Under the prosaic surface of family life in his native city of Columbus, he perceived latent oddities and incongruities which lent themselves to caricature and comic exaggeration. However acerbic his treatment of men and women, he accords canine aberrations a charitable understanding. Like the dogs of E. B. White, with whom Thurber was associated on the staff of* The New Yorker, *Thurber's dogs tend to be earnestly devoted to being helpful. His distinctive and expressive pen and ink drawings of dogs in many situations and moods are an integral part of his commentary on American life. They are generally puzzled, sad, or resigned, as if concurring in Puck's verdict: "What fools these mortals be."*

THE SCOTTY WHO KNEW TOO MUCH

Several summers ago there was a Scotty who went to the country for a visit. He decided that all the farm dogs were cowards, because they were afraid of a certain animal that had a white stripe down its back. "You are a pussy-cat and I can lick you," the Scotty said to the farm dog who lived in the house where the Scotty was visiting. "I can lick the little animal with the white stripe, too. Show him to me." "Don't you want to ask any questions about him?" said the farm dog. "Naw," said the Scotty. "*You* ask the questions."

So the farm dog took the Scotty into the woods and showed him the white-striped animal and the Scotty closed in on him, growling and slashing. It was all over in a moment and the Scotty lay on his back. When he came to, the farm dog said, "What happened?" "He threw vitriol," said the Scotty, "but he never laid a glove on me."

A few days later the farm dog told the Scotty there was another animal all the farm dogs were afraid of. "Lead me to him," said the Scotty. "I can lick anything that doesn't wear horseshoes." "Don't you want to ask any questions about him?" said the farm dog. "Naw," said the Scotty. "Just show me where he hangs out." So the farm dog led him to a place in the woods and pointed out the little animal when he came along. "A clown," said the Scotty, "a pushover," and he closed in, leading with his left and exhibiting some mighty fancy footwork. In less than a second the Scotty was flat on his back, and when he woke up the farm dog was pulling quills out of him. "What happened?" said the farm dog. "He pulled a knife on me," said the Scotty, "but at least I have learned how you fight out here in the country, and now I am going to beat *you* up." So he closed in on the farm dog, holding his nose with one front paw to ward off the vitriol and covering his eyes with the other front paw to keep out the knives. The Scotty couldn't see his opponent and he couldn't smell his opponent and he was so badly beaten that he had to be taken back to the city and put in a nursing home.

Moral: It is better to ask some of the questions than to know all the answers.

SNAPSHOT OF A DOG

I ran across a dim photograph of him the other day, going through some old things. He's been dead twenty-five years. His name was Rex (my two brothers and I named him when we were in our early teens) and he was a bull terrier. "An American bull terrier," we used to say, proudly; none of your English bulls. He had one brindle eye that sometimes made him look like a clown and sometimes reminded you of a politician with derby hat and cigar. The rest of him was white except for a brindle saddle that always seemed to be slipping off and a brindle stocking on a hind leg. Nevertheless, there was a nobility about him. He was big and muscular and beautifully made. He never lost his dignity even when trying to accomplish the extravagant tasks my brothers and myself used to set for him. One of these was the bringing of a ten-foot wooden rail into the yard through the back gate. We would throw it out into the alley and tell him to go get it. Rex was as powerful as a wrestler, and there were not many things that he couldn't manage somehow to get hold of with his great jaws and lift or drag to wherever he wanted to put them, or wherever we wanted them put. He could catch the rail at the balance and lift it clear of the ground and trot with great confidence towards the gate. Of course, since the gate was only four feet wide or so, he couldn't bring the rail in broadside. He found that out when he got a few terrific jolts, but he wouldn't give up. He finally figured out how to do it, by dragging the rail, holding on to one end, growling. He got a great, wagging satisfaction out of his work. We used to bet kids who had never seen Rex in action that he could catch a baseball thrown as high as they could throw it. He almost never let us down. Rex could hold a baseball with ease in his mouth, in one cheek, as if it were a chew of tobacco.

He was a tremendous fighter, but he never started fights. I don't believe he liked to get into them despite the fact that he came from a line of fighters. He never went for another dog's throat but for one of its ears (that teaches a dog a lesson), and he would get his grip, close his eyes, and hold on. He could hold on for hours. His longest fight lasted from dusk until almost pitch-dark, one Sunday. It was fought in East Main Street in Columbus with a large, snarly nondescript that belonged to a big colored man. When Rex finally got his ear grip, the brief whirlwind of snarling turned to screeching. It was frightening to listen to and to watch. The Negro boldly picked the dogs up somehow and began swinging them around his head, and finally let them fly like a hammer in a hammer throw, but although they landed ten feet away with a great plump, Rex still held on.

The two dogs eventually worked their way to the middle of the car tracks, and after a while two or three streetcars were held up by the fight. A motorman tried to pry Rex's jaws open with a switch rod; somebody lighted a fire and made a torch of a stick and held that to Rex's tail, but he paid no attention. In the end, all the residents and storekeepers in the neighborhood were on hand, shouting this, suggesting that. Rex's joy of battle, when battle was joined, was almost tranquil. He had a kind of pleasant expression during fights, not a vicious one, his eyes closed in what would have seemed to be sleep had it not been for the turmoil of the struggle. The Oak Street Fire Department finally had to be sent for—I don't know why nobody thought of it sooner. Five or six pieces of apparatus arrived, followed by a battalion chief. A hose was attached and a powerful stream of water was turned on the dogs. Rex held on for several moments more while the torrent buffeted him about like a log in a freshet. He was a hundred yards away from where the fight started when he finally let go.

The story of that Homeric fight got all around town, and some of our relatives looked upon the incident as a blot on the family name. They insisted that we get rid of Rex, but we were very happy with him, and nobody could have made us give him up. We would have left town with him first, along any road there was to go. It would have been different, perhaps, if he'd ever started fights, or looked for trouble. But he had a gentle disposition. He never bit a person in the ten strenuous years that he lived, nor ever growled at anyone except prowlers. He killed cats, that is true, but quickly and neatly and without especial malice, the way men kill certain animals. It was the only thing he did that we could never cure him of doing. He never killed, or even chased, a squirrel. I don't know why. He had his own philosophy about such things. He never ran barking after wagons or automobiles. He didn't seem to see the idea in pursuing something you couldn't catch, or something you couldn't do anything with, even if you did catch it. A wagon was one of the things he couldn't tug along with his mighty jaws, and he knew it. Wagons, therefore, were not a part of his world.

Swimming was his favorite recreation. The first time he ever saw a body of water (Alum Creek) he trotted nervously along the steep bank for a while, fell to barking wildly, and finally plunged in from a height of eight feet or more. I shall always remember that shining, virgin dive. Then he swam upstream and back just for the pleasure of it, like a man. It was fun to see him battle upstream against a stiff current, struggling and growling every foot of the way. He had as much fun in the water as any person I have known. You didn't have to throw a stick in the water to get him to go in. Of course, he would bring back a stick to you if you did throw one in. He would even have brought back a piano if you had thrown one in.

That reminds me of the night, way after midnight, when he went a-roving in the light of the moon and brought back a small chest of drawers that he found somewhere—how far from the house nobody ever knew; since it was Rex, it could easily have been half a mile. There were no drawers in the chest when he got it home, and it wasn't a good one—he hadn't taken it out of anybody's house; it was just an old cheap piece that somebody had abandoned on a trash heap. Still, it was something he wanted, probably because it presented a nice problem in transportation. It tested his mettle. We first knew about his achievement when, deep in the night, we heard him trying to get the chest up onto the porch. It sounded as if two or three people were trying to tear the house down. We came downstairs and turned on the porch light. Rex was on the top step trying to pull the thing up, but it had caught somehow and he was just holding his own. I suppose he would have held his own till dawn if we hadn't helped him. The next day we carted the chest miles away and threw it out. If we had thrown it out in a nearby alley, he would have brought it home again, as a small token of his integrity in such matters. After all, he had been taught to carry heavy wooden objects about, and he was proud of his prowess.

I am glad Rex never saw a trained police dog jump. He was just an amateur jumper himself, but the most daring and tenacious I have ever seen. He would take on any fence we pointed out to him. Six feet was easy for him, and he could do eight by making a tremendous leap and hauling himself over finally by his paws, grunting and straining; but he lived and died without knowing that twelve- and sixteen-foot walls were too much for him. Frequently, after letting him try to go over one for a while, we would have to carry him home. He would never have given up trying.

There was in his world no such thing as the impossible. Even death couldn't beat him down. He died, it is true, but only, as one of his admirers said, after "straight-arming the death angel" for more than an hour. Late one afternoon he wandered home, too slowly and too uncertainly to be the Rex that had trotted briskly homeward up our avenue for ten years. I think we all knew when he came through the gate that he was dying. He had apparently taken a terrible beating, probably from the owner of some dog that he had got into a fight with. His head and body were scarred. His heavy collar with the teeth marks of many a battle on it was awry; some of the big brass studs in it were sprung loose from the leather. He licked at our hands and, staggering, fell, but got up again. We could see that he was looking for someone. One of his three masters was not home. He did not get home for an hour. During that hour the bull terrier fought against death as he had fought against the cold, strong current of Alum Creek, as he had fought to climb twelve-foot walls. When the person he was waiting for did come through the gate, whistling, ceasing to whistle, Rex walked a few wabbly paces toward him, touched his hand with his muzzle, and fell down again. This time he didn't get up.

T. H. WHITE'S *Brownie*

■ *At mid-century when Terence H. White published his extensive version of the life and fortunes of King Arthur and his court, he made Camelot a part of everyday speech. Probably his two most famous volumes are* The Sword in the Stone *and* The Once and Future King. *At the same time, in his private life, he inclined to solitude. Hence his special sense of loss at the unexpected death of his most cherished companion, Brownie.*

To David A. Garnett

DOOLISTOWN, EIRE
NOVEMBER 25TH, 1944

Dearest Bunny, Brownie died today. In all her 14 years of life I have only been away from her at night for 3 times, once to visit England for 5 days, once to have my appendix out and once for tonsils (2 days), but I did go in to Dublin about twice a year to buy books (9 hours away) and I thought she understood about this. To-day I went at 10, but the bloody devils had managed to kill her somehow when I got back at 7. She was in perfect health. I left her in my bed this morning, as it was an early start. Now I am writing with her dead head in my lap. I will sit up with her tonight, but tomorrow we must bury her. I don't know what to do after that. I am only sitting up because of that thing about perhaps consciousness persisting a bit. She has been to me more perfect than anything else in all my life, and I have failed her at the end, an 180–1 chance. If it had been any other day I might have known that I had done my best. These fools here did not poison her —I will not believe that. But I could have done more. They kept rubbing her, they say. She looks quite alive. She was wife, mother, mistress & child. Please forgive me for writing this distressing stuff, but it is helping me. Her little tired face cannot be helped. Please do not write to me at all about her, for very long time, but tell me if I ought to buy another bitch or not, as I do not know what to think about anything. I am certain I am not going to kill myself about it, as I thought I might once. However, you will find this all very hysterical, so I may as well stop. I still expect to wake up and find it wasn't. She was all I had.

love from TIM

DOOLISTOWN
NOVEMBER 28TH, 1944

Dear Bunny, Please forgive me writing again, but I am so lonely and can't stop crying and it is the shock. I waked her for two nights and buried her this morning in a turf basket, all my eggs in one basket. Now I am to begin a new life and it is important to begin it right, but I find it difficult to think straight. It is about whether I ought to buy another dog or not. I am good to dogs, so from their point of view I suppose I ought. But I might not survive another bereavement like this in 12 years' time, and dread to put myself in the way of it. If your father & mother & both sons had died at the same moment as Ray, unexpectedly, in your absence, you would know what I am talking about. Unfortunately Brownie was barren, like myself, and as I have rather an overbearing character I had made her live through me, as I lived through her. Brownie was my life and I am lonely for just such another reservoir for my love. But if I did get such a reservoir it would die in about 12 years and at present I feel I couldn't face that. Do people get used to being bereaved? This is my first time. I am feeling very lucky to have a friend like you that I can write to without being thought dotty to go on like that about mere dogs.

They did not poison her. It was one of her little heart attacks and they did not know how to treat it and killed her by the wrong kindnesses.

You must try to understand that I am and will remain entirely without wife or brother or sister or child and that Brownie supplied more than the place of these to me. We loved each other more and more every year.

Dear Bunny, I am over the worst, though there is still one thing I can hardly bear to think of. Brownie had immense confidence in me as a doctor and used to come to me for help when she felt an attack coming on. She used to come and look up at me and register being ill. Because I was away, she couldn't do it when she was dying, but she knew she was dying, and went to tell Mrs. McDonagh as a last resource, which failed her. When I think of this my heart is an empty funnel. There is a physical feeling in it. After she was buried I stayed with the grave for one week, so that I could go out twice a day and say 'Good girl: sleepy girl: go to sleep, Brownie.' It was a saying she understood. I said it steadily. I suppose the chance of consciousness persisting for a week is several million to one, but that was the kind of chance I had to provide against. She depended on me too much, and so I had to accept too much responsibility for her. Then I went to Dublin, against my will, and kept myself as drunk as possible for nine days, and came back feeling more alive than dead. She was the only wonderful thing that has happened to me, and presumably the last one. You are wrong that her infertility was due to our relationship. It was the other way round. She adopted me off her own bat, and I took her to the sire at 18 months and several times after, before I cared two straws about her. I also took her to vets, to find out why she flinched at the critical moment, and they said that the passage was malformed. After that, I just used to leave her loose when she was in season. I don't know what I told you before, but I have found out some things. One is that bereaved suicides commit it out of tidyness, not out of grand emotions. Their habits, customs and interests, which means their lives, were bound up with their loved one, so, when that dies, they realise that their own habits etc. are dead. So, as they see that they are dead already, they commit suicide in order to be consistent. Everything is dead except their bodies, so they kill these too, to be tidy, like washing up after a meal or throwing away the empties after a party, and I daresay they find it as tedious. The other thing I have found is that the people who consider too close an affection between men and animals to be 'unnatural' are basing their prejudice on something real. It is the incompatibility

T. H. WHITE 169

of ages. It is in Lucretius. He says that centaurs cannot exist because the horse part would die before the man part. All I can do now is to remember her dead as I buried her, the cold grey jowl in the basket, and not as my heart's blood, which she was for the last eight years of our twelve. I shall never be more than half a centaur now.

I must thank you very, very much for your two letters, which have left me as amazed at your wisdom as I always was at your kindness and information. I have done what you said I was to do, or at any rate I have bought a puppy bitch. Brownie had taught me so much about setters that it seemed silly to waste the education, so I stuck to them. No setter could ever remind me of her, any more than one woman would remind you of another, except in general terms. The new arrangement looks like the foetus of a rat, but she has a pedigree rather longer than the Emperor of Japan's. She is called Cill Dara Something-or-other of Palmerston, but prefers to be called Killie, for lucidity. She nibbles for fleas in my whiskers. We are to accept the plaudits of the people of Erin next St. Patrick's day at the Kennel Club Shew, where we intend to win the Puppy Class and the Novices: in the Autumn we go to watch the Field Trials, which we win the year after. When we have collected 15 points or green stars and can call ourselves CH. in the stud book we are coming to repeat the process in England. We are to have about 4 litters of puppies. Then it is to be America: the camera men & reporters, the drive up Broadway with typists showering us with tape, the reception at the White House, the spotlights at Hollywood. In short, we are determined to make good.

If you really want a Pointer and were not suggesting him in order to encourage me, I will gladly train one for you. . . .

Do you think it would be wrong of me to write a book about Brownie, or that I ought to wait seven years before starting? I have a strong feeling that I want to write it now. . . .

I have joined the Kennel Club as a life member, as I am going to have hundreds and hundreds of setters from now on, to prevent loving one of them too much. When I went to their office about half a dozen dog-like women attended to me so faithfully and gently, and one of them was so exactly like a bull-dog, that I celebrated my entry by crying all over my cheque book. She was solid gold and stood by and gave moral support without speaking. I can't remember whether she barked a bit.

love from TIM

■ *Whatever indifference to animal life Hemingway's enjoyment of bull fights and big game hunting may imply, his treatment of his pets reflects a consistent concern for their well-being. In his home and outbuildings in Cuba in the 1940s numerous cats and dogs were given shelter and food. The most cherished was Black Dog, or Blackie, a faithful spaniel companion for twelve years. Although Hemingway apparently did not commemorate Blackie in any formal way, in this excerpt the bond between the two is confirmed by his wife Mary in her comments on the solace and fidelity the dog provided.*

From HOW IT WAS

Papa [Ernest Hemingway] had been concerned that the cats might feel rejected and hurt if they were moved from the main house. . . . I had never seen him be mean, unkind or less than loving to any of his animals. Animals were love sponges, we knew, and we wanted never to let the sponges go dry. . . .

Making his accustomed rounds of his three or four favorite bars, as much for local news as for booze, Ernest noticed a black springer-looking dog faithfully following. When he walked back to our cabin, the dog followed and Ernest gave him something to eat. Late that night when I opened the back door, I found the dog there, huddled close to the cabin for warmth, and invited him inside. He slept beneath Ernest's bed. All around town and at the Valley we inquired if anyone had lost a black springer spaniel. . . . Nobody knew. Inadvertently or not, someone had left him friendless in Ketchum [Idaho]. Prosaically Ernest named him Blackie and the dog appeared to approve. He accepted me politely and with obedience. He was an Alaskan springer spaniel, Ernest decided. . . .

I was ready to go home, and we prepared to return to Cuba. . . . When he saw luggage dragged out from closets and under beds, Blackie sensed change in the air, and established himself in the front seat of the Buick even before we started packing it and refused to move out, even for food. So I gave him food and affection and assurances in the car, and Ernest murmured, "Don't worry, old boy. You'll come with us." Thirteen days later, walking Blackie in Daytona Beach, I reflected that we had traversed four different zones of place names. . . .

Amidst the joys and surprises of homecoming I was concerned that our other dogs, the band of agreeable but nondescript characters who had gravitated to the Finca [home in Cuba] but lived outside the house, might upset Blackie's introduction to his new domain. Ernest had thought of that. While we were still unloading luggage and I was greeting servants and looking about, he introduced Blackie to the incumbent beasts. I noticed him following some of them around the corner of the garage, Blackie at his heels. Whatever the dog dialogue was, Blackie had to assert his authority only a couple of times before peace reigned. He was a bit bigger than any other dog, and the problem of territory never arose, since little Negrita never challenged his place at Papa's feet, his realm for some twelve years. To us peripheral characters of the household he was always polite, often enchanting. . . .

THURSDAY, SEPTEMBER 1, 1949—06:25

FINCA VIGÍA

"Papa says of the animal situation here at the Finca 'Dogs is trumps but cats is the longest suit we hold'."

Black Dog and Negrita were, meanwhile, flourishing, together with the eight or ten dogs who lived behind the house and on the back staircase leading to the kitchen door. That summer Negrita . . . was attracting all the boy dogs from the neighborhood, frisky-happy with the attention she was receiving, and pretending annoyance when her best friend, Blackie, jealously tried to protect her from the visitors. They both had a dandy summer. . . .

The heat of August ebbed and we were sleeping cool one night in mid-September when I woke up, touched Ernest softly and found he was also awake.

"Been dreaming about H. M. Tomlinson," I murmured. . . .

"Been dreaming about Ford Madox Ford," E. said. "Him, the war."

"We're pretty literary tonight."

"Black Dog—he's been dreaming about Elizabeth Barrett Browning."

"Or about her little dog, what's its name—Ruff? Puff? Fluff?"

We dozed a few minutes. Then E. said, "Flush."

Two-thirds asleep, I tried to remember a famous Hollywood dog who might be the subject of Negrita's dreams, little Negrita sleeping softly on top of the bed between our feet, finally remembered and murmured, "Miss Negrita's dreaming too. Lassie? Negrita never saw a Lassie picture."

"No," said Ernest, muffled in sleep. "Rin Tin Tin." . . .

On January 31 [1953] I noted: "Papa frequently asks Black Dog now, 'Do you think man will survive?' Blackie looks serious. Says Papa, 'He always ponders that question.' "

Other unhappy news came [to us in Paris, 1956] from Cuba. Ernest's devoted Black Dog had died.

Now [the next year in Cuba] he was spending mornings picking gingerly through his records of his early Paris days. . . . He continued missing the company of his faithful Black Dog.

ROBERT FROST'S *Dalmatian Gus*

■ *Although Frost was frequently "out for stars," as he said in another poem, he was rarely out, or in, for dogs. His canine interest lay rather in the constellation Canis Major and particularly in its brightest star, Sirius, in whose eternal presence there were no brevities. Yet on one night, stepping outside his house to see if the Dog Star was keeping his watchful eye on what is "to be gone into," he is diverted by the intrusive visit of a transient Dalmatian who becomes convincingly real through Frost's observation of his canine behavior. Hence what needs "to be gone into" emerges as the relationship of the transient Dalmatian in his house and the eternal "Great Overdog," as he termed Canis Major in another poem. Yet Frost's attempt to make the Dalmatian a symbolic avatar fails, and Frost leaves the conjunction of the heavenly and earthly dogs ambiguous, conceding that even if he should find a "meaning," he would not be inclined to reveal it.*

ONE MORE BREVITY

> I opened the door so my last look
> Should be taken outside a house and book.
> Before I gave up seeing and slept
> I said I would see how Sirius kept
> His watch-dog eye on what remained
> To be gone into if not explained.

But scarcely was my door ajar,
When past the leg I thrust for bar
Slipped in to be my problem guest,
Not a heavenly dog made manifest,
But an earthly dog of the carriage breed;
Who, having failed of the modern speed,
Now asked asylum—and I was stirred
To be the one so dog-preferred.
He dumped himself like a bag of bones,
He sighed himself a couple of groans,
And head to tail then firmly curled
Like swearing off on the traffic world.
I set him water, I set him food.
He rolled an eye with gratitude
(Or merely manners it may have been),
But never so much as lifted chin.
His hard tail loudly smacked the floor
As if beseeching me, "Please, no more,
I can't explain—tonight at least."
His brow was perceptibly trouble-creased.
So I spoke in terms of adoption thus:
"Gustie, old boy, Dalmatian Gus,
You're right, there's nothing to discuss.
Don't try to tell me what's on your mind,
The sorrow of having been left behind,
Or the sorrow of having run away.
All that can wait for the light of day.
Meanwhile feel obligation-free.
Nobody has to confide in me."
'Twas too one-sided a dialogue,
And I wasn't sure I was talking dog.
I broke off baffled. But all the same
In fancy, I ratified his name,
Gustie, Dalmatian Gus, that is,
And started shaping my life to his,
Finding him in his right supplies
And sharing his miles of exercise.

Next morning the minute I was about
He was at the door to be let out

With an air that said, "I have paid my call.
You mustn't feel hurt if now I'm all
For getting back somewhere or further on."
I opened the door and he was gone.
I was to taste in little the grief
That comes of dogs' lives being so brief,
Only a fraction of ours at most.
He might have been the dream of a ghost
In spite of the way his tail had smacked
My floor so hard and matter-of-fact
And things have been going so strangely since,
I wouldn't be too hard to convince,
I might even claim, he was Sirius
(Think of presuming to call him Gus)
The star itself, Heaven's greatest star,
Not a meteorite, but an avatar,
Who had made an overnight descent
To show by deeds he didn't resent
My having depended on him so long,
And yet done nothing about it in song.
A symbol was all he could hope to convey,
An intimation, a shot of ray,
A meaning I was supposed to seek,
And finding, wasn't disposed to speak.

ROBERT SWARD'S *Uncle Dog*

■ *Uncle dog, a garbageman's traveling companion, would seem to be neither a memorable dog nor a young boy's model. Robert Sward's skillful fusion of stanzaic form, imagery, diction, and tone, however, has created a credible canine figure and projected a life-style. The somewhat sophisticated young poet, from whose view uncle dog is described, does not admire uncle dog for any of the standard canine virtues such as loyalty or courage but rather for his ability to live a hedonistic life whereby he escapes all work (especially with garbage) and follows his instincts. He rides on the garbage wagon as free from responsibility as passengers in a chauffeur-driven car. The allusions to automobiles presumably suggest a future when labor will be less irksome. Uncle dog is no heroic Lassie. Instinctively he is a follower of Polonius: "To thine own self be true."*

UNCLE DOG: THE POET AT 9

I did not want to be old Mr.
Garbage man, but uncle dog
Who rode sitting beside him.

Uncle dog had always looked
To me to be truck-strong
Wise-eyed, a cur-like Ford

Of a dog. I did not want
To be Mr. Garbage man because
All he had was cans to do.

Uncle dog sat there me-beside-him
Emptying nothing. Barely even
Looking from garbage side to side:

Like rich people in the backseats
Of chauffeur-cars, only shaggy
In an unwagging tall-scrawny way.

Uncle dog belonged any just where
He sat, but old Mr. Garbage man
Had to stop at everysingle can.

I thought. I did not want to be Mr.
Everybody calls them that first.
A dog is said, Dog! Or by name.

I would rather be called Rover
Than Mr. And sit like a tough
Smart mongrel beside a garbage man.

Uncle dog always went to places
Unconcerned, without no hurry.
Independent like some leashless

Toot. Honorable among scavenger
Can-picking dogs. And with a bitch
At every other can. And meat:

His for the barking. Oh, I wanted
To be uncle dog—sharp, high fox-
Eared, cur-Ford truck-faced

With his pick of the bones.
A doing, truckman's dog
And not a simple child-dog

Nor friend to man, but an uncle
Traveling, and to himself—
And a bitch at every second can.

JAMES DICKEY'S *Dog*

■ *As one of America's most eminent contemporary poets, James Dickey generally bases his poems and fiction on familiar settings, character types, or occurrences—many of them in the South. He makes frequent use of animals and has a special aptitude for involving himself in their feelings, habits, and character. He also frequently utilizes nocturnal settings which nurture subliminal experiences such as his canine transfiguration during the fox chase in the accompanying poem.*

A DOG SLEEPING ON MY FEET

Being his resting place,
I do not even tense
The muscles of a leg
Or I would seem to be changing.
Instead, I turn the page
Of the notebook, carefully not

Remembering what I have written,
For now, with my feet beneath him
Dying like embers,
The poem is beginning to move
Up through my pine-prickling legs
Out of the night wood,

Taking hold of the pen by my fingers.
Before me the fox floats lightly,
On fire with his holy scent.
All, all are running.
Marvelous is the pursuit,
Like a dazzle of nails through the ankles,

Like a twisting shout through the trees
Sent after the flying fox
Through the holes of logs, over streams
Stock-still with the pressure of moonlight.
My killed legs,
My legs of a dead thing, follow,

Quick as pins, through the forest,
And all rushes on into dark
And ends on the brightness of paper.
When my hand, which speaks in a daze
The hypnotized language of beasts,
Shall falter, and fail

Back into the human tongue,
And the dog gets up and goes out
To wander the dawning yard,
I shall crawl to my human bed
And lie there smiling at sunrise,
With the scent of the fox

Burning my brain like an incense,
Floating out of the night wood,
Coming home to my wife and my sons
From the dream of an animal,
Assembling the self I must wake to,
Sleeping to grow back my legs.

■ *When Ackerley's* My Dog Tulip *was published, it was acclaimed by some of his contemporaries as the finest book about a dog ever written. This verdict evidently derives from the book's precise observation of canine behavior and recognition of the impingement of human codes on a dog's instinctive impulses. Readers of Ackerley's* Letters *will be aware of how closely the fictional Tulip resembles his dog Queenie. In his treatment of both Ackerley fused objectivity and empathetic solicitude.*

From MY DOG TULIP

My dog is an Alsatian bitch. Her name is Tulip. Alsatians have a bad reputation; they are said to bite the hand that feeds them. Indeed Tulip bit my hand once, but accidentally; she mistook it for a rotten apple we were both trying to grab simultaneously. We all make mistakes and she was dreadfully sorry. She rolled over on the grass with all her legs in the air; and later on, when she saw the bandage on my hand, she put herself in the darkest corner of the bedroom, and stayed there for the rest of the afternoon.

I could do with her whatever I wished—except stop her barking at other people. Yet she behaved always with exemplary dignity and good breeding wherever she went, so long as she was let alone. Her sweetness and gentleness to myself were such that it was almost impossible for me to believe that those were not the prevailing characteristics of her nature; but the language she used to others certainly sounded pretty strong.

It is necessary to add that she is beautiful. People are always wanting to touch her, a thing she cannot bear. Her ears are tall and pointed. Her face also is long and pointed, basically stone-gray but the snout and lower jaw are jet black. And in the midst of her forehead is a kind of Indian caste-mark, a black diamond suspended there. A shadow extends across her forehead from either side of this caste-mark, so that, in certain lights, the diamond looks like the body of a bird with its wings spread, a bird in flight. A delicate white ruff, frilling out from the lobes of her ears, frames this strange, clownish face, and covers the whole of her throat and chest with a snowy shirt front. . . .

My disinclination to visit vets was in frequent conflict with my need to consult them. Tulip looked too thin; beneath her sable tunic all her ribs were visible. The distressing word "Worms" was dropped into my ear by a kind acquaintance, and soon afterwards I decided to take her to see Miss Canvey, the lady vet. Alone in the surgery I listened apprehensively for sounds—screams from Miss Canvey, cries of pain or rage from Tulip. But the place was as silent as the grave. Then the door opened and Tulip reappeared, this time with Miss Canvey in tow. "How did she behave?" I asked, while Tulip cast herself into my arms and lavished upon me a greeting more suitable in its extravagance to lovers who had been parted for years. "Good as gold," said Miss Canvey. "You're the trouble. She's in love with you, that's obvious. And so life's full of worries for her. She has to protect you; that's why she's upset when people approach you. But when you are not there, there's nothing for her to do, of course, and no anxiety." . . .

Tulip never let me down. She is nothing if not consistent. She knows where to draw the line, and it is always in the same place, a circle around us both. Indeed, she is a good girl but—and this is the point—she would not care for it to be generally known. When, therefore, the little local boys ask me, as they often do, in their respectful and admiring way, though mistaking Tulip's gender: "Does he bite, Mister?" I always return the answer which she, and Miss Canvey, would wish me to give. . . .

A cousin of mine, aware that I had been looking in vain for accommodation that would accept an Alsatian dog, invited us down [to "Mon Repos," her country home in Sussex] to stay. Tulip was enjoying herself: why not leave her there to profit from the wonderful sea air and come down myself at weekends to join her? I consented.

An alarm clock woke me at 6:45 every Monday morning. Tulip, who slept always in my room, would get up too and follow me about as I tip-toed between bedroom, bathroom and kitchen. I knew, without looking at her, that her gaze was fixed unswervingly upon me, that her tall ears were sharp with expectation. Avoiding her eyes for as long as I could, I would go about my preparations; but the disappointing had to be done at last. As I picked up my bag in the bedroom, she would make her little quick participating movement with me through the door, and I would say casually, as though I were leaving her for only a moment, "No, old girl, not this time." No more was needed. She would not advance another step but, as if the words had turned her to stone, halt where she was outside the bedroom door. Now to go without saying goodbye to her I could not, though I knew what I should see, that stricken look, compounded of such grief, such humility, such despair, that it haunted me all the journey up [to London]. "Goodbye, sweet Tulip," I would say and, returning to her, raise the pretty disconsolate head that drooped so heavily in my hands, and kiss her on the forehead. Then I would slip out into the darkness. But the moment the door had closed behind me she would glide back into our bedroom, which was on the front of the bungalow, and rearing up on her hind legs at the window, push aside the curtains with her nose and watch me pass. This was the last I would see of her for five days, her gray face, like a ghost's face, at the window, watching me pass. . . .

For what seemed an incredible length of time she showed no sign at all of the coming event. Then quite suddenly, I observed the swell and sag of her belly and, in the first days of May, she began to flag and to take rests during our walks. Soon Putney Common was as far as she could go, and even on these short strolls she would quietly halt and sink down upon the cool grass. Stretching myself beside her, I would smoke and read until she felt able to continue.

I asked Miss Canvey to be on hand in case we needed her, but Tulip took us unawares. She whelped five days before her scheduled time. It was a marvellous sight, to me very affecting; but I think to anyone who did not know and love her as I did, it must have been a solemn and moving thing to see this beautiful animal, in the midst of the first labor of her life, performing upon herself, with no help but unerringly, as though directed by some divine wisdom, the delicate and complicated business of creation. . . .

Once over the road we are among trees and bracken, lost to the world of dogs and men. Here, where the silver trees rise in their thousands from a rolling sea of bracken, Tulip turns into the wild beast she resembles. Especially at this early hour the beautiful, remote place must reek of its small denizens, and the scent throws her into a fever of excitement. Round and round she goes, rhythmically rising and falling, like a little painted horse in a roundabout, her fore-legs flexed for pouncing, her tall ears pricked and focused, for she has located a rabbit in a bush. She must be everywhere at once. She must engirdle the crafty, timid creature and confuse it with her swiftness so that it knows not which way to turn. And barking is unwisdom, for it hinders her own hearing of the tiny, furtive movement in the midst of the bush. Silently, therefore, she rises and falls, like a dolphin out of the green sea among the silver masts, herself the color of their bark, battling her wits with those of her prey. The rabbit can bear no more and makes its dart; in a flash, with a yelp, she is after it, streaking down the narrow track. Rabbits are agile and clever. But Tulip is clever too. She knows now where the burrows lie and is not to be hoodwinked. The rabbit has fled downhill to the right; she sheers off to the left, and a tiny scream pierces the quiet morning and my heart. Alas, Tulip has killed. I push through the undergrowth to the scene of death. She is recumbent, at breakfast. . . .

How cruel a trick, I think, to concentrate, like a furnace, the whole of a creature's sexual desire into three or four weeks a year. How can I put her from me? She is my friend, an honoured member of my household. Years of devotion, years of habit, bind us together. It is true that she is now more amiable to strangers than is her wont, but as I think of that I remember also her desperate, her frenzied agitation whenever she loses sight of me in the streets. I cannot send her from me. And how can I tamper with so beautiful a beast? Yet I *am* tampering with her. I am frustrating her. Must I have this recurrent nightmare forever? And is it my imagination that the more I frustrate her the more protracted, the more insistent, her heats become? As though Nature were saying: "You escaped me last time. You shall not escape me this!" . . .

It is autumn, it is spring. . . . The birch woods, and she is off upon her errands, I upon mine. The solitary place belongs to us. It is our private garden, our temple, our ivory tower. The illusion of happiness, of peace, must have continuity, must have permanence. I look down into the grove where the great birch tree stands. It is the heart of the woods, the sacred precinct, and with Tulip beside me I descend into it. The place belongs to us. I know many of its secrets now, many of its joys and sorrows. Tulip is adding to the latter; I regret it, but love is cruel. It pleases her to chase and kill; she must have her pleasure. She must have everything she wants, except the thing she needs. While she persecutes, I protect; thus may I balance the accounts, perhaps, hers and mine, and propitiate the tutelary god.

■ *From his early days as a writer Steinbeck confessed his need for the companionship of dogs. In 1933 after the death of his Tillie, or as he said "properly Tylie Eulenspiegel," he noted in his* Letters *that she "haunts the house terribly" and that he dreamed of dogs sitting in a circle about him, every one of which he wanted. He soon purchased an Irish terrier.*

From TRAVELS WITH CHARLEY: IN SEARCH OF AMERICA

I took one companion on my journey—an old French gentleman poodle known as Charley. Actually his name is Charles le Chien. He was born in Bercy on the outskirts of Paris and trained in France, and while he knows a little poodle-English, he responds quickly only to commands in French. Otherwise he has to translate, and that slows him down. He is a very big poodle, of a color called *bleu,* and he is blue when he is clean. Charley is a born diplomat. He prefers negotiation to fighting, and properly so, since he is very bad at fighting. Only once in his ten years has he been in trouble—when he met a dog who refused to negotiate. Charley lost a piece of his right ear that time. He is a good friend and traveling companion and he contributed much to the trip. A dog, particularly an exotic like Charley, is a bond between strangers. Many conversations en route began with "What degree of a dog is that?" . . .

Now, Charley is a mind-reading dog. He knows we are going long before the suitcases come out, and he paces and worries and whines and goes into a state of mild hysteria, old as he is. During the weeks of preparation he was underfoot the whole time and made a damned nuisance of himself. He took to hiding in the truck, creeping in and trying to make himself look small.

Charley is a tall dog. As he sat in the seat beside me, his head was almost as high as mine. He put his nose close to my ear and said, "Ftt." He is the only dog I ever knew who could pronounce the consonant *F*. This is because his front teeth are crooked; because his upper front teeth slightly engage his lower lip Charley can pronounce *F*. The word "Ftt" usually means he would like to salute a bush or a tree.

Charley likes to get up early, and he likes me to get up early too. And why shouldn't he? Right after his breakfast he goes back to sleep. Over the years he has developed a number of innocent-appearing ways to get me up. He can shake himself and his collar loud enough to wake the dead. If that doesn't work he gets a sneezing fit. But perhaps his most irritating method is to sit quietly beside the bed and stare into my face with a sweet and forgiving look on his face; I come out of deep sleep with the feeling of being looked at. But I have learned to keep my eyes tight shut. If I even blink he sneezes and stretches, and that night's sleep is over for me. Often the war of wills goes on for quite a time, I squinching my eyes shut and he forgiving me, but he nearly always wins. . . .

In establishing contact with strange people, Charley is my ambassador. I release him, and he drifts toward the objective, or rather to whatever the objective may be preparing for dinner. I retrieve him so that he will not be a nuisance to my neighbors—*et voilà!* A child can do the same thing, but a dog is better. I sent out my ambassador and drank a cup of coffee while I gave him time to operate. Then I strolled to the camp to relieve my neighbors of the inconvenience of my miserable cur. The dog had caused no trouble, he [the chieftain] said. The truth was that he was a handsome dog. I, of course, found myself prejudiced in spite of his deficiencies, but the dog had one advantage over most dogs. He was born and raised in France. . . .

I started into Chicago long before daylight. Rocinante [the truck camper] was whisked away to a garage for storage. Charley had to go to a kennel to be stored, bathed, and Hollanderized. Even at his age he is a vain dog and loves to be beautified, but when he found he was to be left out in Chicago, his ordinary aplomb broke down and he cried out in rage and despair. I closed my ears and went away quickly to my hotel.

Charley was torn three ways—with anger at me for leaving him, with gladness at the sight of Rocinante, and with pure pride in his appearance. Charley's combed columns of legs were noble things, his cap of silver blue fur was rakish, and he carried the pompom of his tail like the baton of a bandmaster. A wealth of combed and clipped moustache gave him the appearance and attitude of a French rake of the nineteenth century. He sat straight and nobly in the seat of Rocinante and he gave me to understand that while forgiveness was not impossible, I would have to work for it.

He is a fraud and I know it. And I know for a fact that five minutes after I had left Charley he had found new friends and had made his arrangements for his comfort. But one thing Charley did not fake. He was delighted to be traveling again, and for a few days he was an ornament to the trip. . . .

Only through imitation do we develop towards originality. Take Charley, for example. He has always associated with the learned, the gentle, the literate, and the reasonable both in France and in America. And Charley is no more like a dog than he is like a cat. His perceptions are sharp and delicate and he is a mind-reader. I don't know that he can read the thoughts of other dogs, but he can read mine. Before a plan is half formed in my mind, Charley knows about it, and he also knows whether he is to be included in it. I know too well his look of despair and disapproval when I have just thought that he must be left at home. . . .

Whatever my purpose in going to Yellowstone, I'm glad I went because I discovered something about Charley I might never have known.

A pleasant-looking National Park man checked me in and then he said, "How about that dog? They aren't permitted in except on leash."

"Why?" I asked.

"Because of the bears."

"Sir," I said, "this is a unique dog. He does not live by tooth or fang. He respects the rights of cats to be cats although he doesn't admire them. He turns his steps rather than disturb an earnest caterpillar. His greatest fear is that someone will point out a rabbit and suggest that he chase it. This is a dog of peace and tranquility. I suggest that the greatest danger to your bears will be pique at being ignored by Charley. I'll lock him in the back, sir. I promise you Charley will cause no ripple in the bear world, and as an old bear-looker, neither will I."

Less than a mile from the entrance I saw a bear beside the road, and it ambled out as though to flag me down. Instantly a change came over Charley. He shrieked with rage. His lips flared, showing wicked teeth that have some trouble with a dog biscuit. He screeched insults at the bear, which hearing, the bear reared up and seemed to me to overtop Rocinante. Frantically I rolled the windows shut and, swinging quickly to the left, grazed the animal, then scuttled on while Charley raved and ranted beside me, describing in detail what he would do to that bear if he could get at him. A little farther along two bears showed up, and the effect was doubled. Charley became a maniac. Where did he learn it? For the first time in his life Charley resisted reason, even resisted a cuff on the ear. He became a primitive killer lusting for the blood of his enemy. Bears simply brought out the Hyde in my Jekyll-headed dog. . . .

I drove across the upraised thumb of Idaho. I was having to make many stops for Charley's sake. Charley was having increasing difficulty in evacuating his bladder. Not only did he hurt, but his feelings were hurt. I looked up a veterinary in the phone book and rushed Charley into the examination room. When a stranger addresses Charley in baby talk, Charley avoids him. For Charley is not a human; he's a dog, and he likes it that way. He feels that he is a first-rate dog, and has no wish to be a second-rate human. When the alcoholic vet touched him with his unsteady, inept hand, I saw the look of veiled contempt in Charley's eyes. . . .

I was in New Orleans; I bought a poor-boy sandwich and got out of town. Weariness flagged me down and I stopped at a pleasant motel, but I could not sleep. I had not felt one moment free from the tension. Everyone, white and black, lived in it and breathed it. I tossed about until Charley grew angry with me and told me "Ftt" several times. But Charley doesn't have our problems. He doesn't belong to a species clever enough to split the atom but not clever enough to live in peace with itself. He doesn't even know about race, nor is he concerned with his sister's marriage. I've seen a look in dogs' eyes, a quickly vanishing look of amazed contempt, and I am convinced that basically dogs think humans are nuts. . . .

My own journey started long before I left and was over before I returned. It is very strange. Up to Abingdon, Virginia, I can reel back the trip like film. After Abingdon—nothing. Rocinante leaped under my heavy relentless foot. If you think I am indulging in fantasy about the trip, how can you explain that Charley knew it was over too? He at least is no dreamer, no coiner of moods. He went to sleep with his head in my lap, never looked out of the window, never said "Ftt," never urged me to a turn-out. If that doesn't prove the truth of my statement, nothing can.

DAVID WAGONER'S *Retriever*

■ *During the past generation David Wagoner has been consistently one
of America's most skillful and rewarding poets. He is especially adept at
fusing creature and setting into a brief, unified, and lucid poetic statement.
Here in a one-sentence vignette of a runaway retriever the dog's fugitive
and frantic uneasiness is revealed entirely through his behavior, appearance, and environment.*

GOLDEN RETRIEVER

Dew-soaked and bleary-eyed with the smells of the field,
He zigzags out of cheatgrass and wild roses
And fallen thistles, as gold, as ragged, his tongue
Lolling, nose high, his breath trailing a mist
Over the empty weed crowns as he drinks in
The whole morning at once, around his neck
A broken chain that follows him over hummocks,
By sunlight on the sheen of cobwebs binding
The dead spikelets of grass and their living stems,
And down through sedge and rushes along the creek,
And up among brambles and arches of blackberry
To disappear in the light-filled field again.

■ *Merwin is one of contemporary America's most lucid and thoughtful poets—a notably conscious stylist in both his poems and prose. His favorite American writer is Thoreau, with whom he shares a concern for American culture and values. In writing of Ali he reflects much of the devotion, delight, and sadness intertwined in the canine-human bond.*

ALI

Small dog named for a wing
never old and never young

abandoned with your brothers on a beach
when you were scarcely weaned

taken home starving
by one woman with
too many to feed as it was

handed over to another
who tied you out back in the weeds
with a clothesline and fed you if she remembered

on the morning before the eclipse of the moon
I first heard about you over the telephone

only the swellings of insect bites
by then held the skin away from your bones

thin hair matted filthy the color of mud
naked belly crusted with sores
head low frightened silent watching

I carried you home and gave you milk and food
bathed you and dried you

dressed your sores and sat with you
in the sun with your wet head on my leg

we had one brother of yours already
and had named him for the great tree of the islands
we named you for the white shadows
behind your thin shoulders

and for the reminder of the desert
in your black muzzle lean as an Afghan's

and for the lightness of your ways
not the famished insubstance of your limbs

but even in your sickness and weakness
when you were hobbled with pain and exhaustion

an aerial grace a fine buoyancy
a lifting as in the moment before flight

I keep finding why that is your name

the plump vet was not impressed with you
and guessed wrong for a long time
about what was the matter

so that you could hardly eat
and never grew like your brother

but played with him as long as you could
oh small dog wise in your days

never servile and never disobedient
and never far
watching and listening

standing with one foot on the bottom stair
wanting it to be bedtime

standing in the doorway looking up
tail wagging slowly below the sharp hip bones

finally you were with us whatever we did
intelligent dignified uncomplaining
fearless loving
and dying

the gasping breath through the night
ended an hour and a half before daylight

the gray tongue hung from your mouth
we went on calling you holding you

feeling the sudden height

Source Notes

PAGE

1   Alexander Pope, *Pope's Minor Poems*, ed. Norman Ault and John Butt, Twickenham edition of Pope's *Works*, vol. VI (New Haven: Yale University Press, 1964).

5   John Gay, *Poems*, vol. II (London: Muses Library, 1893).

7   Oliver Goldsmith, *The Vicar of Wakefield*, ed. Arthur Friedman, *Collected Works* (Oxford: Oxford University Press, 1966).

9   William Cowper, *Works of William Cowper*, ed. Robert Southey (London: Baldwin and Cradock, 1837).

12   James Fenimore Cooper, *The Prairie* (New York: Dodd Mead & Co., 1954).

17   Thomas Campbell, *Poetical Works* (London: E. Moxon, 1854).

19   William Wordsworth, *Poetical Works* (New York: Thomas Y. Crowell & Co., n.d.).

23   Sir Walter Scott, *Familiar Letters of Sir Walter Scott* (Boston: Houghton Mifflin & Co., 1894); "Death of Camp" from J. G. Lockhart, *Memoirs of the Life of Sir Walter Scott*, vol. I (Philadelphia: Carey, Lea, & Blanchard, 1837).

26   Lord Byron, *Poetical Works* (New York: Thomas Y. Crowell & Co., n.d.).

28   John Clare, *The Shepherd's Calendar* (London: Oxford University Press, 1964).

32   Charles Lamb, *Letters*, ed. E. V. Lucas (New Haven: Yale University Press, 1935).

34   Charles Dickens, *Oliver Twist*, ed. Kathleen Tillotson (Oxford: Oxford University Press, 1966).

41   "A Friend Not Literary, and Other Friends" from John Forster, *Walter Savage Landor* (Boston: Fields, Osgood & Co., 1869); "Giallo" from Walter Savage Landor, *Poems, Dialogues in Verse, and Epigrams*, ed. Charles G. Crump (London: J. M. Dent & Co., 1903).

46   Abraham Lincoln, *The Collected Works of Abraham Lincoln*, vol. I, ed. Roy P. Basler (New Brunswick: Rutgers University Press, 1953).

50   Elizabeth Barrett Browning, "Flush or Faunus" from D. Hewlett, *Elizabeth Barrett Browning, a Life* (New York: Alfred A. Knopf, 1952); letters to Robert

Browning from *The Letters of Robert Browning and Elizabeth Barrett Barrett, 1845–1846,* vols. I, II, ed. Elvan Kintner, (Cambridge, Mass.: Belknap Press of Harvard University Press, 1969); letters to Miss Mitford from *Letters of Elizabeth Barrett Browning* (New York: Macmillan Co., 1897).

57 E. C. Gaskell, *Life of Charlotte Brontë* (New York: D. Appleton and Co., 1857).

60 Emily Dickinson, *Letters of Emily Dickinson,* ed. T. H. Johnson and Theodora Ward (Cambridge, Mass.: Belknap Press, 1958).

63 Dr. John Brown, *Spare Hours, First Series, Rab and His Friends and Other Papers* (Boston: Houghton Mifflin, 1883).

67 Eleanor Atkinson, *Greyfriars Bobby* (New York: Harper & Bros., 1912).

75 Fred Gipson, *Old Yeller* (New York: Harper & Bros., 1956).

83 John Muir, "An Adventure with a Dog and a Glacier," *The Century Magazine,* vol. LIV (September 1897).

95 Matthew Arnold, *Poetical Works* (London: Oxford University Press, 1950).

98 William Faulkner, *Go Down, Moses* (New York: Random House, 1942).

103 Jack London, *The Call of the Wild* (New York: Grosset & Dunlap, n.d.).

109 Mark Twain, *Complete Stories of Mark Twain,* ed. Charles Neider (Garden City, N.Y.: Hanover House, 1957).

114 Anna Hempstead Branch, *The Shoes That Danced* (Boston: Houghton Mifflin, 1905).

116 John Galsworthy, *The Inn of Tranquility* (New York: Charles Scribner's Sons, 1912).

124 Edgar Lee Masters, *Spoon River Anthology* (New York: Macmillan & Co., 1916).

125 Harold Monro, *Georgian Poetry, 1918–1919,* vol. IV, ed. Edward Marsh (New York and London: Poetry Bookshop, 1920).

127 Carl Sandburg, *Early Moon* (New York: Harcourt Brace, 1930).

128 Loren Eiseley, *The Night Country* (New York: Charles Scribner's Sons, 1971).

130 Thomas Hardy, from "Winter Words" in *Collected Poems* (New York: Macmillan & Co., 1952).

132 Irene Rutherford McLeod, *A Book of Poetry,* ed. Edwin Markham (New York: W. H. Wise & Co., 1927).

133 John S. O'Brien, *By Dog Sled for Byrd* (Chicago: Thomas S. Rockwell Co., 1931).

138 Alexander Woollcott, *Long, Long Ago* (New York: Viking Press, 1943).

143 E. B. White, "A Boston Terrier" in *One Man's Meat* (New York: Harper & Bros., 1944); "Bedfellows" in *Essays* (New York: Harper & Row, 1977).

151 Eric Knight, *Lassie Come-Home* (Chicago: John C. Winston, 1940).

158 Gertrude Stein, *Paris France* (New York: Charles Scribner's Sons, 1940); and *Wars I Have Seen* (New York: Random House, 1945).

162 James Thurber, "The Scotty Who Knew Too Much" from *Fables For Our Time* (Harper & Bros., 1940); and "Snapshot of a Dog" from *The Thurber Carnival* (New York: Harper & Bros., 1945).

167 T. H. White, *The White-Garnett Letters,* ed. David A. Garnett (New York: Viking Press, 1968).

171   Mary Welsh Hemingway, *How It Was* (New York: Alfred A. Knopf, 1976).

174   Robert Frost, *In the Clearing* (New York: Holt, Rinehart & Winston, 1962).

177   Robert Sward, *Kissing the Dancer* (Ithaca, N.Y.: Cornell University Press, 1957).

179   James Dickey, *Drowning with Others* (Middletown, Conn.: Wesleyan University Press, 1962).

181   J. R. Ackerly, *My Dog Tulip* (New York: Fleet Publishing Co., 1965).

185   John Steinbeck, *Travels with Charley: In Search of America* (London: Pen Books, Ltd, 1971).

189   David Wagoner, "Golden Retriever," *The New Yorker* (10 August 1981).

190   W. S. Merwin, "Ali," *Iowa Review,* 13 (1982).

COPYRIGHT ACKNOWLEDGMENTS

An abridgment of "Bedfellows" from *Essays of E. B. White*. First appeared in *The New Yorker*. Copyright © 1956 by E. B. White. Reprinted by permission of Harper & Row, Publishers, Inc.

Adaptation of excerpts from *Lassie Come-Home* by Eric Knight.Copyright 1940 by Jere Knight; copyright renewed 1968 by Jere Knight, Betty Noyes Knight, Winifred Knight Mewborn, and Jenny Knight Moore. Reprinted by permission of Curtis Brown Ltd.

Excerpt from *Wars I Have Seen* by Gertrude Stein. Copyright 1945 by Random House, Inc. Reprinted by permission of Random House, Inc., and the Estate of Gertrude Stein.

"The Scotty Who Knew Too Much" from *Fables for Our Time* by James Thurber. Copyright 1940 by James Thurber; copyright renewed 1968 by Helen Thurber. (First published in 1940 by Harper & Row, Publishers, Inc.) Reprinted by permission of Helen Thurber.

"Snapshot of a Dog" from *The Middle-aged Man on the Flying Trapeze* by James Thurber. Copyright 1935 by James Thurber; copyright renewed 1963 by Helen W. Thurber and Rosemary T. Sauers. (First published in 1935 by Harper & Row, Publishers, Inc.) Reprinted by permission of Helen Thurber.

Excerpt from *The White-Garnett Letters* edited by David Garnett. Copyright © 1968 by David Garnett and the Executors of the Estate of the late T. H. White. Reprinted by permission of Viking Penguin Inc. and David Higham Associates Limited.

Excerpt from *How It Was* by Mary Hemingway. Copyright 1951, © 1955, 1963, 1966, 1976 by Mary Hemingway. Reprinted by permission of Alfred A. Knopf, Inc., and Weidenfeld & Nicolson Ltd.

"One More Brevity" from *The Poetry of Robert Frost*, edited by Edward Connery Lathem. Copyright 1953, © 1962 by Robert Frost; copyright © 1969 by Holt, Rinehart and Winston. Reprinted by permission of Holt, Rinehart and Winston, Publishers, the Estate of Robert Frost, and Jonathan Cape Ltd.

"Uncle Dog: The Poet at 9" from *Kissing the Dancer & Other Poems* by Robert Sward (Cornell University Press, 1964) and from *Poems: New & Selected (1957–1983)* (AYA Press, Toronto, 1983). Copyright © 1983 by Robert Sward. Reprinted by permission of Robert Sward.

"A Dog Sleeping on My Feet" from *Drowning with Others* by James Dickey. Copyright © 1962 by James Dickey. The poem first appeared in *Poetry*. Reprinted by permission of Wesleyan University Press.

Excerpt from *My Dog Tulip* by J. R. Ackerley. Copyright © 1965 by J. R. Ackerley. Reprinted by permission of Fleet Press Corporation, New York City.

Excerpts from *Travels with Charley* by John Steinbeck. Copyright © 1961, 1962 by the Curtis Publishing Co.; copyright © 1962 by John Steinbeck. Reprinted by permission of Viking Penguin Inc., McIntosh & Otis, Inc., and William Heinemann Limited.

"Golden Retriever" from *First Light* by David Wagoner. Copyright © 1981 by David Wagoner. The poem first appeared in *The New Yorker*. Reprinted by permission of Little, Brown and Company in association with the Atlantic Monthly Press.

"Ali" from *Opening the Hand* by W. S. Merwin. Copyright © 1983 by W. S. Merwin. Reprinted by permission of Atheneum Publishers.